T0305166

The Legal Foundations of Micro-Institutional Performance

We dedicate this work to the late, great 'troublesome economists' from Michigan State University including Dave Schweikhardt, Warren Samuels and Al Schmid, without whose dedication to ideas, debate and teaching this body of work would never have manifested or persisted.
We remember the legacy of each, every time we endeavor to question the status quo.

The Legal Foundations of Micro-Institutional Performance

A Heterodox Law & Economics Approach

Sarah S. Klammer

Economist and Academic Specialist, Extension Center for Local Government Finance and Policy, Department of Agricultural, Food and Resource Economics, Michigan State University, USA

Eric A. Scorsone

Director and Associate Professor, Extension Center for Local Government Finance and Policy, Department of Agricultural, Food and Resource Economics, Michigan State University, USA

Edward Elgar
PUBLISHING

Cheltenham, UK • Northampton, MA, USA

Published by
Edward Elgar Publishing Limited
The Lypiatts
15 Lansdown Road
Cheltenham
Glos GL50 2JA
UK

Edward Elgar Publishing, Inc.
William Pratt House
9 Dewey Court
Northampton
Massachusetts 01060
USA

A catalogue record for this book
is available from the British Library

Library of Congress Control Number: 2022931164

This book is available electronically in the **Elgar**online
Economics subject collection
http://dx.doi.org/10.4337/9781802204339

ISBN 978 1 80220 432 2 (cased)
ISBN 978 1 80220 433 9 (eBook)

Printed and bound by CPI Group (UK) Ltd, Croydon, CR0 4YY

Contents

PART II   APPLICATIONS

Figures

Tables

Preface

When the 2020 global coronavirus pandemic hit, the world witnessed the relative effectiveness (or ineffectiveness) of many of its largest organizations in real time. Suddenly the working rules, recommendations and laws of the World Health Organization and each country's respective health organizations became the subject of daily mass-market news coverage, and the interdependence at play between international, national and local systems became clear. The rules that were promulgated in this period including social distancing, facial masks, large gathering restrictions, business and facility space limitations and closures gave us a new appreciation for links between human decision making, public health and the economy. These rules impacted all of us, often unequally, making the importance of ongoing study into the implications of rules and institutions such as these clear.

While overwhelming, the existence and makeup of each of these working rules influenced the course of COVID-19 globally and in each specific geography. The differing formal and informal institutions around the world shaped the outcomes between countries and locales that we are just now beginning to dig into. Different rules mean different outcomes. Praise, criticism and calls for institutional change are already in motion at every level of government.

All of this begs the question: If the makeup of institutions is so important, so vital to the outcomes themselves, why don't we spend more time learning about them? And, perhaps more importantly, with so little understanding of the makeup and functioning of institutions, what makes us think we are so capable of selecting the "right" institutions? If recent economic failures have shown us anything, it is that economic science is not nearly so precise as we often claim, and institutional choice can have large and far-reaching unintended consequences. This book seeks to provide a language for economists and economic analysts to examine and investigate the implications of the institutional and legal foundations of the economy at a micro-institutional level so that we might better anticipate some of these consequences.

Sarah S. Klammer and Eric A. Scorsone

East Lansing, MI, August 2021

Acknowledgements

We acknowledge the valuable contributions of many heterodox groups engaged in facilitating discussion around modern issues of neoliberalism and the path forward. While too numerous to list, we thank you for your efforts to illuminate the way. We thank you also for the encouragement you offer to scholars, new and old, in tackling their own passion projects in the intersection of law, policy and economics.

Eric Scorsone also wants to thank his family for putting up with this long process, and colleagues at Michigan State University and many other locations from whom he has learned so much. He also wants to thank the work of Sarah to come on board at Michigan State University and put in two long years of effort to make this project a reality. Finally, he wants to acknowledge the Starbucks staff on Lake Lansing Road in Lansing, MI for the hours put in there to write this book.

Sarah Klammer thanks several colleagues and friends (including Simone, Alex R, Alex G, Byron, Chris, and her mother), for their support and comments throughout the writing process. She also thanks Eric for his support of the project and efforts as co-author, as well as several of Michigan State University Department of Agricultural, Food and Resource Economics' former and current graduate students for kicking ideas around with her before the draft had even begun. As always, to God be the glory.

All errors and omissions in this book remain our own.

Introduction: Institutional law and economics

> [The] rights which individuals possess, with their duties and privileges, will be to a large extent what the law determines. As a result, the legal system will have a profound effect on the working of the economic system and may in certain respects be said to control it. (Coase, 1991, p. 10)

The fields of law and economics, as well as institutional economics more generally, have developed somewhat separately from the rest of the economics field. How these fields emerged and became distinct involves a lengthy lesson in the evolution of a field made up of many moving parts, each with very different ideas about what they should be working towards. Complicating this is that many of economics' purveyors are often not economists at all (including some of our most recognized and acclaimed). This complicated history and the resulting factions of the present day can give students the idea that institutions (or more narrowly, rules and law), are something separate from standard economic theory that can be picked up in an elective course if one has the time. And we increasingly do not seem to have the time.

In Robin Matthews' 1986 presidential address to the Royal Economic Society, a definition common to all major approaches to the study of institutions was offered: "[institutions are] sets of rights and obligations affecting people in their economic lives" (Matthews, 1986). He further stated that a body of thinking had evolved based on two propositions: (1) that institutions do matter and (2) the determinants of institutions are susceptible to analysis by tools of economic theory.

Matthews outlined what he saw as the central concepts surrounding institutions emerging during this period, namely the handling of property rights and transaction costs by the economics field, institutions as conventions and norms of economic behavior and institutions as types of contracts in use with questions about authority or who decides what (and later, who gets what). We recognize these key concepts in multiple sub-disciplines taught today: law and economics, behavioral and organizational economics, social choice and welfare economics.

Indeed, today those with little formal institutional economics training, or those who would not identify themselves as institutional economists, conduct the most "institutional" economic work. Awards have been given in the area of behavioral and organizational economics (such as those to Kahneman, Smith, Ostrom and Thaler, among others), inextricably tied to the study of institutions. In Nobel Laureate Elinor Ostrom's first book, *Governing the Commons* (1990), she stressed the importance of cultivating an understanding of institutions (no easy feat):

> Instead of presuming that optimal institutional solutions can be designed easily and imposed at low cost by external authorities, I argue that "getting the institutions right" is a difficult, time-consuming, conflict-invoking process. It is a process that requires reliable information about time and place variables as well as a broad repertoire of culturally acceptable rules. New institutional arrangements do not work in the field as they do in abstract models unless the models are well specified and empirically valid and the participants in a field setting understand how to make the new rules work.

Other scholars made similar observations. A. Allan Schmid, an agricultural economist from Michigan State University, devoted much of his career to developing a model for institutional impact and change analysis. Almost two decades prior to Ostrom's famous work, he called for the development of an analytical institutional economics, or models that could assist with clarifying the institutional variables:

> One gets the feeling that [certain new policies and institutions] are preferred more out of recognition that what exists has failed some of the environmental interest groups rather than any solid prediction that the alternative will produce a given new result when actually implemented in detail. Before we can improve our predictive powers we will need to develop further an analytical institutional economics. (Schmid, 1972, p. 893)

Ostrom's observations of the difficulties of "getting the institutions right" and Schmid's call for the development of an "analytical institutional economics" are the practical confirmation of the long-ago observation of Nobel Laureate Ronald Coase.[1] Coase argued in 1960 that any system of property rights is capable of leading to Pareto efficiency provided it is a "complete system" – one where all rights to all the benefits from all scarce resources are imputed to someone and are tradeable. However, Coase added that a complete system is never possible because of transaction costs and that some incomplete systems (i.e. some institutions) are more conducive to Pareto efficiency than others. Even after his work became widely recognized, Coase lamented that, "My point of view has not in general commanded assent, nor has my argument, for the most part, been understood." and that "Exchange [in economics] takes place without any specification of its institutional setting. We have consumers without humanity, firms without organization, and even exchange without markets" (Coase, 2012).

Even before Coase and his famous work, others in the legal field were thinking in a similar fashion. Yale Law professor Wesley Hohfeld wrote in 1913 (expanded somewhat in 1917) about the need to clarify the legal concepts of many economic and social relations and the fundamental interrelationship between economic agents. Hohfeld felt that many legal scholars and judges were unclear in their writing and thinking regarding basic concepts such as rights and duties. He set out to create a matrix of rights and other associated "jural relations," such as duties, immunities, liabilities, powers and disabilities. The point of this Hohfeldian scheme was to clarify and create an understanding that each relationship or situation between parties had to be examined carefully to determine where one party's right existed, under what conditions and who was on the other end. The second major point of Hohfeld's work as it applies to economic transactions is that this correlative relationship or interdependence is fundamental and does not only exist under voluntary agreements.

More recently, economists of the institutional law and economics tradition have argued similar points. The first point, in line with Hohfeld, is that the distribution of rights, duties, privileges and immunities is absolutely essential to the ultimate distribution of income, wealth and overall economic performance (and vice versa). The natural extension of this point is that (1) interdependence between agents in the economy is fundamental and ubiquitous and (2) coercion and power play a critical role in understanding economic performance.

Warren Samuels of Michigan State University called the combination of these realities the "legal–economic nexus." The nexus is the fact that law drives economic performance and in turn economic performance drives the law and legal change. Samuels writes:

> efficiency in the sense of Pareto optimality means the exhaustion of gains from trade of goods. But efficient-optimal allocations are specific to the definition and assignment of rights forming the basis on which trades take place. There is no unique optimal result, only rights-structure-specific optimal results. Moreover, *efficiency* in the Pareto sense cannot dispositively be applied to the definition and assignment of rights themselves, because efficiency requires an antecedent determination of the rights. (Samuels, 2007: 23–24)

Schmid and Daniel Bromley (University of Wisconsin) have expressed the same point of the legal–economic nexus with different language and terminology. Schmid, in his work with Samuels, discussed the fact that each institutional structure results in a distinct set of economic outcomes including costs to the various parties. They wrote:

> cost involves a reciprocal relationship. It is often said that in an argument that such and such a policy will incur a cost, as if incurring of a cost is dispositive of the issue at hand ... The difference has to do with whose interests are to become a cost to whom else. (Samuels and Schmid, 2005, p. 167)

Bromley, in his book *Economic interests and institutions* (1989) uses the example of worker safety within a mine to make this same point. He explains that laws that promote mining safety mean that the mining company will spend less on producing minerals and more on ensuring a mining design that is safer for employees. The economic performance result is more safety and less mine output. The lack of mining safety law would imply the inverse result. We are back, once again, to a common question: Whose interests count?

The reality described by Coase, Hohfeld and all those related to the school of institutional law and economics is that institutions, and more specifically the law, cannot be separated from the study of economics. Standard neoclassical models and approaches may treat the legal framework in which all economic actors operate as exogenous to the model in the interest of ease of use and often also necessity. But these assumptions, their limitations and parameters must be well understood. When we conduct any economic analysis (especially impact analysis), without domain knowledge about the operationalization of variables, mechanism, etc., we run the risk of drawing misleading conclusions at best and useless or damaging conclusions at worst. We would be hard pressed to find an academic that has not encountered such a misguided paper or article at some point in their career.

The implications of a world in which institutions operate perfectly and without friction is that there could be no transaction costs, no unpleasant distributional issues. All rights and responsibilities would be well defined, accepted and not subject to changing behavior and the evolving needs and wants of individuals and society as a whole. We might go as far as to say that people in this world could no longer be interdependent. But the reality of the world we live in is that people *are* interdependent, constantly in a state of either conflict or cooperation. Institutions, and the markets they make up, don't function smoothly in any kind of natural or devised state and they are always changing. Models that take this into account – that really get at the institutional variable(s) – allow economists (and other analysts) to reshape their analysis to account for how legal systems and specific legal rules impact economic performance and outcomes.

This kind of institutional awareness is needed now more than ever. It is our hope that by the end of the text, the reader should come away with a better understanding of how to conduct a positive analysis of the regularities in behavior and subsequent performance that will emerge from a set of rules, as well as the ability to specify those sets of rules.

WHAT TO EXPECT FROM THIS TEXT

In this text, we borrow common ground and the foundational elements necessary from both law and economics literature to introduce and apply a method of institutional impact analysis centered on the idea of human interdependence. Most law and economics textbooks seek to apply economic concepts and analysis to understanding the law. Given that law provides a critical foundation to the operation and distribution of wealth and resources across the economy, our goal is to reverse-engineer this standard approach and provide economists with the legal concepts and tools that can be applied in economic analysis.

The specific aim of this text is to introduce advanced undergraduate and graduate students to some concepts that will allow them to understand how to apply legal concepts to their analyses. This novel approach to law and economics has only been developed in a few relatively obscure journal articles over the past few decades. While we will cite and use much institutional economics literature, this text does not attempt to be a one-stop-shop for those interested in learning about institutional economics and institutionalist traditions. Many excellent texts and articles exist that cannot all possibly be consolidated and explored here. Rather, we provide a practical resource for those interested in analyzing what agents can do with differing institutional structures (the 'rules of the game').

To this end, the text adopts and further develops the legal framework of scholar Wesley Hohfeld as an analytical tool for economists to incorporate into economic analysis. This analytical tool provides specific direction in identifying the rights, duties, liberties and exposure to the acts of each other as economic agents. We build this framework onto an existing model of institutional impact analysis called the Situation-Structure-Performance (SSP) framework as developed by A. Allan Schmid.

The SSP model for institutional change and for institutional impact analysis focused on building a strong awareness of the fundamental issues of human conflict and cooperation, its root sources and the consequences of the methods we choose to address such human interdependence. We take the solid foundations of Schmid's model as embodied in his books *Property, Power, and Public Choice* (1987) and *Conflict and Cooperation: Institutional and Behavioral Economics* (2004), and rework it to include a more formalized accounting of legal structure, in the hope of making it more easily applied. The resulting model is one still centered on interdependence, but much more grounded in Hohfeldian legal foundations of rights and duties and all that come with them. We call this the Legal-Economic Performance (LEP) framework.

Broadly, the model works by starting with the identification of an economic situation where agents are interacting with or in interdependence with one another. The Hohfeldian framework is used to identify the status quo and understand the current structure of legal relations. Once the analyst has identified a situation of interdependence, the next step is to identify the institutional (legal) options available to address the interdependence. This is where the analyst considers all of the possible alternatives that are available and the Hohfeldian language of legal structure and legal change come into play. Finally, the third part of our new framework is the determination of economic performance outcomes from the intersection of the situational and structural components outlined above.

The text is divided into two parts. Part I contains four chapters devoted to developing the foundational ideas and tools central to the LEP framework. Once this framework is developed, we then apply the framework to a variety of legal cases and examples in Part II.

Chapter 1 begins by framing institutions and developing a concrete language for how to discuss them. Much of what is commonly referred to as institutional economics deals with the organizing of human interaction and social order – or conflict and cooperation. The consequences and relevance of interdependence are topics at the core of economic literature. In this chapter, we take a particular view of how to approach interdependence that borrows heavily from the Great Lakes School of Institutional Economics and the legal–economic nexus as embodied by scholars such as Warren Samuels and A. Allan Schmid. Much of the material, therefore, is heterodox in scope.

In Chapter 2, we develop the language of interdependence using the terminology of Hohfeldian jural relations. To our knowledge, this is the first time the work of Hohfeld has been integrated into a formal economic framework. It will certainly be the first time most economics students have been asked to frame economic transactions with thought to legal theory. With this in mind, we provide only a simplified version of how jural relations might be applied to economic impact analysis. The possibilities and varied styles of applications beyond this text remain to be discovered. Chapter 3 builds onto the Hohfeldian relations introduced in Chapter 2 to discuss ideas of property and more complex legal relations.

Chapter 4 combines institutional foundations from Chapter 1 and legal terminology from Chapters 2 and 3 into the Legal-Economic Performance Framework. All parts of the model are discussed in this chapter, along with guided examples applying concepts to simplified examples.

In Part II of the text, we apply this framework to various real-world (though modified) examples (one per chapter). The hope is that these will be useful both for learning in the classroom as well as for training the mind to think in a new way. The text ends, like most economics textbooks, with a conclusion followed by a section of appendices to expand on topics mentioned briefly in the main text.

NOTE

1. The Coase Theorem was not in fact developed by Coase but by George Stigler. There are many versions of the Coase Theorem today. The original Stigler version basically states that in a world of zero transaction costs, the initial distribution of property rights does not matter as the economic agents will negotiate until economic efficiency is reached.

PART I

Institutions, law and economics

1. Institutions

Imagine that you live in a home with a long driveway flanked by several large, beautiful cedar trees. These trees have stood before your home longer than you have lived in it. Maybe you appreciate them on a day-to-day basis. Maybe you hardly notice they are there. Either way, they are part of your property, with all that entails. They may provide shade for your cars, shade for a garden or habitat for the pollinators and birds that you enjoy. Maybe they do little but drop needles and branches that you have to clean up. Either way, the cedar trees are yours.

Now imagine that you receive a letter. In this letter, you are informed that your cedar trees pose a pest risk to the apple trees another resident in your town cultivates several miles away. As such, the city has declared that all cedar trees within a certain radius of apple orchards be cut down, including yours.

A scenario like this took place for homeowners across Virginia in 1914. The conflict originated with a rust disease that travels from ornamental cedars (where it is harmless) to apple trees (where it is damaging). The Virginia legislature passed a statute that allowed apple growers to petition the state entomologist to investigate and destroy without compensation any offending cedars. One such landowner, Miller, owned a large stand of ornamental red cedar trees on his property in Shenandoah County, Virginia. Schoene, the Virginia state entomologist, ordered Miller to cut down his red cedar trees pursuant to the Cedar Rust Act of Virginia. Miller fought back, ultimately taking the case all the way to the United States (U.S.) Supreme Court. In *Miller et al.* v. *Schoene* (1928), the Court ruled that the state legislature had the right to order the removal of cedar trees grown within a certain vicinity of local apple growers (Miller), relying on the state entomologist (Schoene) to determine the risk cedar rust posed to the apple industry (see Appendix A for a brief overview of the case).

This case is but one example of the many kinds of decisions courts make every day. When there is a conflict between parties or individuals, as there often is when rules and laws are unclear about who has rights and how they are to be carried out, someone or something must sort it out. How this is done or whose desk the decision falls on varies across jurisdictions and types of situations. In the U.S., there is a system of higher and lower courts for sorting out issues of rights, and the *Miller* (1928) case progressed all the way to the top.

It is easy to read the above example and identify the preliminary conflict in the case as one between one property owner and another. The cedar owner has not done anything "wrong" to justify the destruction of his trees, just as the orchardist has done nothing to bring about this pathogenic plight that might destroy his apple crop. Yet the existence of the others' property, and a lack of clear definition of certain aspects of their property rights, has created friction between the two.

In cases like this, we might say that it is appropriate for one of our institutions to serve as mediator, to deliver justice and keep the peace most effectively. Much like the real result of *Miller* (1928), however, state mediation results in winners and losers. The court might have been attempting to maximize the societal good to the best of its ability when valuing the health of the apple trees above the value of the potentially damaging cedar trees, but at the end of the day the cedar owner lost their trees through no fault of their own. Were the courts to instead wash their hands of the issue or to "let the market decide," as we so often hear espoused, we would still face a similar issue of assigning winners and losers – this time based on status quo property laws that favor the cedar owner.

When individuals analyze policy outcomes or attempt to propose new policy, properly identifying winners and losers is imperative. To do this, it is necessary that those conducting the analysis or proposing change have an understanding of where the current distribution of rights comes from, and how that might change perceptions of performance. In the *Journal of Law and Economics* in 1971, Warren Samuels used the case of *Miller* (1928) to argue that there was a strong relationship between law and economics. In that article, Samuels articulated a core proposition of the School of Institutional Law and Economics, "the issue is not government or no government but which interests, that is, whose interests the state is used to effectuate" (Samuels, 1971). In this article and subsequent writings,[1] Samuels used this case to highlight the issue of human interdependence, and the role of institutions in sorting it all out.

In this chapter, we will work to provide a solid base for working with and understanding this institutional variable and the issue of human interdependence. We start with a brief overview of institutions and institutional analysis in the Great Lakes tradition with its focus on human interdependence before introducing a useful taxonomy for talking about institutions moving forward. The chapter concludes with further discussion of human interdependence and how it might be used as the unit of observation for our analysis. Look for "Think about it" boxes throughout this text that attempt to connect ideas to real scenarios or interesting hypotheticals as an aid to thinking about these complex issues.

1.1   THINKING ABOUT INSTITUTIONS

Economists, when thinking about how consumers make choices about what to buy, imagine them consulting their utility function and wallet. They also imagine the producer picking up the recipe on how to produce something and assessing the cost of inputs and the price of outputs in deciding what, where and how much to make. Every time a consumer goes to purchase a product or service, an institutional set of rules underlies that transaction. The consumer, without perhaps even knowing it, by engaging with a seller/producer is interdependent with that other party in terms of legal rules and in many cases informal rules as well. The transaction, if it takes place in the U.S., will likely be subject to some version of the Uniform Commercial Code. This code specifies rights, duties and powers for the various economic agents. The code helps shape the options, opportunities and choices of both consumers and producers. Institutions such as these are ubiquitous in our everyday decision making.

We know that particular institutions, such as well-defined and secure property rights, rule of law and political constraints, matter for economic development. We also know that institutions matter for our more day-to-day interactions, whether it be applying for a loan or the process of getting a driver's license. Even the market itself, which none of us can claim could matter more than it does in all aspects of our lives, is an institution made up of many complex rules and relations.[2] In short, institutions are everywhere. Developing a sense of them and a method for breaking them down and discussing them is a crucial first step toward beginning to understand and make decisions involving their structure and development.

Despite their importance (or perhaps because of it), there continues to be little agreement or widespread adoption of any one definition of institutions and what they might be or how they may be described, in the field of economics in particular. A brief survey of the literature of the past two decades on the topic makes this clear (see Hodgson, 2006, 2019). Rather than attempt to develop a comprehensive theory of institutions, in this section we provide a brief overview of the definition and characteristics of institutions that are necessary for beginning to cultivate an awareness and language of institutions for the purposes of conducting institutional impact analysis.

1.1.1   Defining Institutions

Institutions go by many names and are examined throughout the literature from many angles, ranging from extremely broad definitions that include any kind of social convention to narrow definitions of formal rule-making bodies. The *New Institutional Economics* handbook defines institutions as "the written and unwritten rules, norms and constraints that humans devise to reduce uncertainty and control their environment" (Menard and Shirley, 2005; North, 1991). Thorstein Veblen defined institutions as "a way of thought or action of some prevalence and permanence, which is embedded in the habits of a group or the customs of a people" (Hamilton, 1932, p. 84). John R. Commons called institutions "collective action in control, liberation, and expansion of individual action" (Commons, 1950, p. 21). North's definition is more specific, identifying both formal and informal institutions: "the formal rules (constitutions, statute and common law, regulations, etc.), informal constraints (norms of behavior, conventions, and internally imposed rules of conduct), and the enforcement characteristics of each" (North, 1994). Taken together, these definitions paint a rather broad picture of institutions as both internalized processes of decision making or externalized means of social ordering, or sometimes both. This can make breaking into the study of institutions difficult, often seeming tautological and overly academic.

In a paper devoted to understanding and defining institutions and some of the struggles of their discussion, Hodgson describes institutions as "the kinds of structures that matter most in the social realm: they make up the stuff of social life" (Hodgson, 2006). He continues,

> The increasing acknowledgement of the role of institutions in social life involves the recognition that much of human interaction and activity is structured in terms of overt or implicit rules. Without doing much violence to the relevant literature, we may define institutions as systems of established and prevalent social rules that structure social interactions. Language, money, law, systems of weights and measures, table manners, and firms (and other organizations) are thus all institutions. (Hodgson, 2006, p. 2)

This definition fits with those of the original institutional economists, Commons and Veblen. Both understood institutions as special types of social structure with the potential to modify individuals as well as their more internalized preferences or purpose. A. Allan Schmid modified this general definition in terms of human relationships and paired with it some properties for Hohfeldian legal analysis (which we introduce in Chapter 2), to define institutions as **"sets (networks) of ordered relationships (connections) among people that define their rights, their exposure to the rights of others, their privileges, and their responsibilities"** (Schmid, 2004, p. 6).[3] It is to this definition that we will continually refer and build from in this text.

Schmid's definition of institutions includes both the formal relationships legislated and sanctioned by the state that we are accustomed to thinking about as well as the informal, tacit and internalized rights that similarly influence our actions (habits of tipping, basic ideas of honesty, etc.). His definition encourages us to think of institutions not as something that exist *a priori*, but as systems of relations between individuals and groups, constantly changing and modifying each other (Schmid, 2004; Potts, 2000). This focus on institutions as relationships allows us to build a balanced framework of institutional impact analysis focused on the reciprocal nature of human interdependence.

Schmid's definition builds on the premise of individuals and institutions as separable, but interdependent and evolving entities. Individuals shape institutions and institutions shape individuals (Hodgson, 1999). An institution is not something apart from individuals, but rather the system of individuals and the reality of their interdependence. Grasping this concept is important to avoid the conception of individual versus government when the issue is really individual A (or group of individuals A) versus individual B (or group of individuals B) (Schmid, 2004, pp. 8–9). We discuss the evolutionary process of institutions in more depth in Section 1.1.4.

Sets of ordered relationships are embedded in each other to form complex systems where different levels are both interdependent and mutually defined (Schmid, 2004, p. 6). The relationships of individuals at firm level are part of relationships among firms in an industry that in turn make up the larger economy. Each set, or level, is simultaneously informed or influenced by those in others. For instance, a dress code developed at a workplace would be influenced by both the prevailing social norms of society at the time as well as higher-level rules (such as certain non-discrimination laws), as well as individuals' sense of their relationship with (or responsibilities to) these other parties. The chosen dress code then becomes part of the set. The formation of informal habits follows a similar course.

These relationships can be described through a language of rights, privileges and responsibilities. Whether formal or informal, they can be broken down into a language of rights that makes it clear what one can do or not do in regards to both individual action but also in regards to modifying or forging new rules or relationships. In the above dress code example, for instance, you would likely have access to a written document detailing what you may or may not wear, alongside some sort of policy as to the consequences of not following the code. Your responsibilities as an employee (to follow the code) and the employer's (to enforce) are clear. You might also choose to modify the relationship by quitting, and would likely follow some process to do so based on the informal or formal rules that matter to you (i.e. the social norm of giving two weeks' notice or some rule that dictates formal written notice within x period).

1.1.2 Institutions Help Define Opportunity Sets (Define and Enable and Constrain Choices)

The concept of constraints is introduced in most economics courses along with the general concept of opportunity sets, or the choices that are available to you.

Typically, there is the introduction of a budget constraint, consumer preferences and firm technology that serve to shape the available choice or opportunity set for consumers and producers. The consumer has certain stronger feelings for one consumption bundle over another but can only buy so much subject to how much money or resources they have available now or in the future. At the same time, the firm's choices about what and how much to make and at what price are shaped by technology and cost of inputs. Within these constraints and preferences, consumers and producers have to make choices.

In fact, there are a number of other factors that play into the consumer and producer choice sets and the focus here is on those of the institutional variation. The institutional makeup of the economy makes an enormous difference in the shape of these choice or opportunity sets in addition to prices, technology and preferences. As Ronald Coase (1991) stated in his Nobel Laureate speech, "As a result the legal system will have a profound effect on the working of the economic system and may in certain respects be said to control it."

We all have interests and make claims, but they are limited by our opportunity sets. Only a small subset of these are sanctioned (enforced) by society. These socially or otherwise enforceable claims are otherwise known as rights[4] (Bromley, 1991). The details of such are included in various levels of institutions, most obviously the written word of codes and contracts. They can be broken down into complex sets of jural relations between agents. Bromley (2010) describes institutions as sets of dual expectations. These two-sided relationships consist of:

1. Rules: what participants may/must/must not do.
2. Expectation: of the rule by economic participants.
3. Enforcement/remedies: of the rule by a collective entity.

Following Bromley, the usefulness and persistence of institutions largely boils down to their ability to structure social interactions by creating stable expectations of the behavior of others. Institutions enable ordered thought, expectation and action by imposing form and consistency on human activities in the form of rules (Hodgson, 2006). In economics, we call these rules constraints, but a constraint for one person can also be an opportunity for another. In this way, institutions more generally define opportunity sets. These opportunity sets influence what physical things we can put together to create new things, or more broadly what actions we take in the marketplace and out. Thus, institutions simultaneously define and constrain opportunity sets, for you and all those you engage with.

An institution can be thought of as a structured human relationship – or a situation of interdependence. This relationship is often described in terms of rules and positions that define opportunity sets. In thinking of institutions as sets of dual expectations as Bromley describes, this becomes clear: rules can be defined as "if X, do Y (or don't do Y), under conditions Z." If Alpha possesses physical ownership of an item X, they have the right to its use without interference, Beta must not interfere, under expectation of the rule and other context of the specific situation (the legal structure, enforcement, etc.) and vice versa. The thing of interest here is not the relationship between Alpha and the object, which is a matter of the physical production function, but rather the implied relationship between Alpha and Beta. The ownership relationship translates as Beta avoids certain acts relative to a physical commodity. This is the source of Alpha's opportunities (Schmid, 2004). If Alpha owns a forest, in most jurisdictions Beta may not go and chop down all the hardwood on the parcel. Alpha may do so, or not do so, or use the land and timber for any number of purposes that Beta has no say in. This applies to many types of "goods," including those that are less tactile. In *Miller* (1928), we see a dispute where cedar growers are told orchardists have greater priority and therefore right to their production over that of the cedar owners. If cedar owners were to continue production as before, they would have to find a way to buy out or convince the orchardists to cede that right in some way. They could also move or plant something else, but this too is now an additional cost to be borne by one party. Their opportunity set has changed as a result of the new ruling laid out by the courts.

When we specify an institution in terms of institutional structure, it is shorthand for a relationship, situation of interdependence and opportunity set. It is this dual or multi-sided nature of rules that sets the stage for human conflict and cooperation. This conception does not start with an unlimited field of action that is then constrained. It starts with human interdependence to be sorted out (Schmid, 2004).

1.1.3 Institutions Inform Performance

Much of the work of economists, administrators, government officials and other researchers involves some kind of impact analysis, often of proposed changes in written rules or requirements. When those making rules or proposing alternative institutional structures do not understand how particular combinations of rules may impact or change actions and outcomes in the downstream environment, rule changes may produce unexpected outcomes (Ostrom, 2005, 2008; Schmid, 2004, 2006). This makes a solid foundation in institutions and the measurement of their performance important for any individual involved in the social sciences, whether you are formally conducting an impact analysis or not.

Institutions structure performance at every level of social action. Consider the U.S. Constitution. In the Constitution, rules are outlined that influence the process for making laws: who can participate, how they might go about it, what they might or might not consider. That process influences the laws and other rules we use in our everyday lives (who gets to vote, who gets to drink, access to affordable healthcare, etc.). Even organizational rules within a workplace, at stores frequented or within services used define the possible performance outcomes available to individuals.

The impact of alternative institutions on performance is made obvious through cases like *Miller* (1928). The owners of the two types of trees discovered an interdependence that neither was previously aware of, and each party petitioned the respective institutions in place to sort it out for them. The apple growers used the Virginia legislature to secure their right to a disease-free environment, meaning that the cedar trees were cut. The cedar owners then used the courts to attempt to reverse this outcome, ultimately failing. Rights were assigned to the orchardists. Had the decision gone the other way, or the courts reversed the decision, the new institutional structure would have yielded a performance favorable to the cedar owners (but perhaps less favorable to society, as determined by the courts).

There is often a demand for science to supply an answer to the question, "What is the best institution?" This question is difficult, if not impossible to answer. Everything that we have to work with, all the existing outcomes and experiences, are based on layers and layers of institutions. As in *Miller* (1928), whether we could say that institutions are effective or produce a desirable performance outcome is very much up to whose interests we deign to count.

Consider some of the potential institutional alternatives you might evaluate. For example, what are the consequences of single-payer healthcare versus a multi-payer system? What about marginal cost pricing versus average cost pricing rules? Whose interests count when deciding between publicly owned utilities versus private? Public versus alternative financing of education? Public versus private charity? Who gets what goods and services under these alternatives? At what cost? Choosing one institutional alternative over another means making choices about who gets what, or the performance of the situation. A single-payer healthcare system obviously has different performance outcomes than a multi-payer system, or of other institutional alternatives for paying for healthcare costs. An institutional structure where the male head of the household is the only voice considered in the political process will likely have different outcomes on a myriad of issues than one where all adults regardless of gender or of household status have a voice. But what does this mean for our analyses?

Consider the classic example of the Pigouvian tax on emissions of a local factory. Residents of the area are unhappy with the current air pollution, some reporting declining health as a result of inhaling the smog, others complaining of the general damage to the vista and environment. The crux of the issue quickly becomes one of who has rights to the air: is it the residents, who wish to breathe clean air, or the factory owners, who wish to continue emitting to maximize production? To do nothing is not a neutral choice; it results in the breathers effectively having no rights to their desired quality of air while the factory owners gain all the rights. To give air rights to the residents similarly skews performance in the other direction, with breathers gaining all the power to determine quality and the factory owners none of it. The solution has often been for the government to introduce a tax equal to some calculation of the external marginal cost (the social cost of pollution) in an effort to restore pollution to what would be called a "market-efficient" level. This too, however, is choosing a specific level of performance that has both winners and losers.

We might similarly think of these issues in cap and trade programs with how permits are allocated, the grandfathering of firms and other distributional effects. The use of permit programs can protect important resources, but depending on how they are designed some stakeholders will benefit over others. For instance, the auctioning of emissions permits can be used as an effective way to distribute permits to those with the most resources to use, often generating revenues for conservation and related projects in the process. But this system automatically favors those who can afford to pay the most. Some economists may say this is efficient, but it is still introducing a new institutional structure (permit auctioning) that chooses winners and losers.

In the field of economics there are many common ways for measuring performance between two alternatives. Efficiency, Pareto optimality and minimized transaction costs are the dominant interrelated concepts most often referenced. None of these measures are naturally objective, and all fall prey to their assumptions when used without awareness and caution.

One of the classic contenders for measuring performance is efficiency. Can we test institutional alternatives by which one is more efficient? The short answer is no. We might be able to say which institutional alternative is most efficient at achieving the interest of Alpha or Beta, but we must specify which first. Efficiency is a derivative of the institutional choice, not the other way around. Even "efficient" institutional changes that reduce transaction costs or increase productivity or economic growth may do so only at the expense of certain individuals or groups (Rutherford, 1994, p. 161). For instance, if some policy reduces transaction costs for the majority group (say, one already established in an industry), but raises them for new entrants, transaction costs may be lowered overall, but that does not make it satisfactory or efficient for the group now facing heightened barriers. Similarly, the existing system of high transaction costs may have benefited a group of middle-men or negotiators whose job was to navigate it on behalf of the firms. The change may be "efficient" for some, but not others.

The concept of market efficiency in equilibrium is similarly fraught. Consider the standard idea of economic demand, where demand is a function of willingness (and ability) to pay (WTP). What is WTP for a water treatment plant built to serve extremely poor citizens in India? Part of this calculation might depend on citizens' opportunity cost (lost wages), of illness avoided. By definition, if citizens are poor, then wages are low and WTP is low. If these are low, and the cost of the plant exceeds this number, then the project could be called "inefficient" and would not be provided. By standard economic training, an allocation of resources that maximizes total surplus is efficient. In this case no firm can produce the plant at a cost low enough to meet or fall below citizens' WTP. Production of the good is therefore zero. These are the kinds of issues in which those in development economics are well versed. In developing countries, it is impossible to ignore the impacts of institutions on economic performance and individual well being. Under alternative institutions that foster higher wages, for instance, WTP will increase and the most efficient point will change again.

As Schmid (2004) wrote,

> The problem with efficiency is that there are too many of them and thus efficiency gives no basis for choosing among them. We are necessarily comparing efficiency $E1$ with efficiency $E2$. Within each there is of course a set of efficient and inefficient outcomes. This just says that once you decide whose interests count, stick to it. But that says nothing about choosing $E1$ or $E2$. That takes a moral choice of whose interests count.

To summarize, efficiency is a normative concept that is based on measures of economic performance (prices, quantity produced, etc.) under one set of rules (institutions) and/or versus another.

In other words, institutions have different levels of performance, and the implications of this characteristic cannot be ignored in economic analysis. To address this challenge, the performance of alternative institutions could be specified in substantive terms of outcomes for all stakeholders. This allows the analyst to avoid normative bias while still giving each interest the information necessary to answer the question of what is good for them. In later chapters, we will talk more about other measures of performance of institutional alternatives, like minimizing transaction costs and the Coase Rule.

1.1.4   Institutions Evolve

Like the individuals who create and form them, institutions are constantly evolving. As individuals and societal preferences evolve and change, so do the rules and systems we put in place to address them. Existing institutions shape individuals and individual actions may again modify either formal or informal institutions. In this way, institutions are subject to a self-feedback loop, where a change in institutions triggers changes downstream that may eventually change the original institution yet again.

This self-feedback loop makes the aspect of time crucial for the purposes of properly specifying the institutional variable. We can think of institutions in the context of the long term and the short term. Over the long term, institutions are forward looking (Commons, 1959) and endogenous to their context, meaning they reflect behavior (Aoki, 2007). This is visible in Figure 1.1, where conduct leads to new outcomes that again feed back into higher-level institutions and characteristics of the world. For example, mask mandates during the COVID-19 pandemic led to greater incidence of mask wearing in the U.S., a higher level of which continues even as the mandates have expired. This behavioral change could no doubt become a new norm (or level of acceptableness) that feeds into the current institutional structure at some future point in time. Researchers may look (and undoubtedly already are looking) into this change via institutional change analysis.

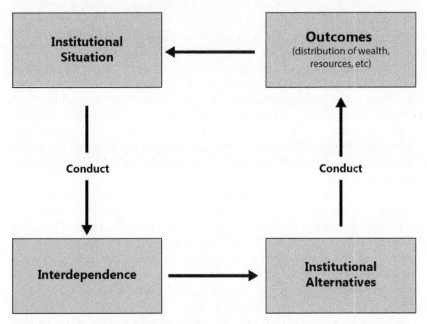

Figure 1.1   Institutional change

Institutions play a role in mental models (or ways of thinking) in the long term. Hodgson (2007) reminds us of the arguments of original institutionalists that transmission of information from institution to individual is impossible without a coextensive process of enculturation. Enculturation is defined as the process through which the individual learns the meaning and value of sense data that are communicated. This is similar to the process Denzau and North (2000) explore, where the role of mental models, ideologies and institutions shape choices and outcomes that determine political and economic performance.[5] They describe mental models as the internal representation that individual cognitive systems create to interpret the environment (shaped by culture, experience, etc.), and ideologies as the shared framework of mental models that groups of individuals possess that provide both an interpretation of the environment and a prescription as to how that environment should be structured. In this way, mental models and ideologies understandably shape the way individuals take in and process information, ultimately influencing their choices.

For instance, the mask mandate in the example above undoubtedly constrained some individuals' behavior. Changed behavior then leads to new or modified interdependence, which may or may not be subject to an impact analysis if modification of structure is desired. Behavior (or conduct) is not simply one part of the model.[6] Over the short term, institutions shape behavior by constraining our choices or opportunity sets (as discussed in Section 1.2). The resulting conduct informs the kind of situation creating interdependence (and often the reasonable structural alternatives we have available). Conduct, along with all those upstream details, then again influences how our alternatives play or may play out, as shown in Figure 1.1. These outcomes then inform those upstream variables in the long term. Behavior drives this evolutionary process. Both the short-term constraints and the long-term processes explored briefly above should make it clear that analyses and explanations of social (economic) issues cannot be institution free, but must be brought into the analysis from the beginning.

Consider for a moment a proposed change in some policy or structure. Presumably, the goal of a proposed change in policy is to elicit some kind of change in human behavior, leading to a more desirable result. The effectiveness of the change depends on how effectively its mechanism works with existing evolutionary processes. If the new structure does not account for existing upstream modifiers of human behavior and interdependence, it is likely to be poorly matched or ill conceived. Similarly, if the researcher does not have a realistic behavioral model or data with which to predict subsequent conduct of agents after the change, the predictive power of the entire analysis will be limited.

Especially over time, institutions may evolve in both intentional and unintentional ways. In some cases, especially with informal institutions or cultural rules, no person(s) specifically intends to create a certain rule. The rule evolves as people act in a certain manner and others begin to follow and act in a similar manner. On the other side, some concerted efforts to modify outcomes via structural changes *do not* result in a change, or the desired change, in conduct or subsequent performance. Each instance could be explained with the right kind of analysis, either institutional change analysis (long term) or institutional impact analysis (near term), though perhaps not to satisfaction for numerous reasons.

Though institutions are created and modified by individuals, saying much about the effectiveness of aggregating individual preferences to this process is much more difficult. Depending on the distribution of those rights and responsibilities we referenced earlier, or the distribution of power in a society more generally, not everyone's ideologies or everyone's choices are valued equally or carry the same weight in the existing societal and legal structure of a locale. The process is always more effective for some. Not as effective for others. The evolution of all things in the social realm will continue, regardless of issues of distribution or disparities between the perceived value of certain ways of thinking or doing.

There is also the issue of path dependence, or positive feedback of social processes. North (1990) explores how the standard characteristics of increasing returns in technology can be applied to institutions. In contexts of complex social interdependence, new institutions will often entail high fixed or start-up costs, and involve considerable learning effects, coordination effects and adaptive expectations. In institutionally dense environments, initial actions (such as pursuing and receiving an expensive college degree) push individual behavior onto paths that are hard to reverse. As social actors make commitments based on existing institutions and policies, the cost of exit from existing arrangements generally rises dramatically (Pierson, 1997). Political processes in particular are one area where sequencing may be critical, where early choices matter more than later ones (Pierson, 2000).

Both of these realities are important to remember when conducting a survey of the present institutional structure, or when working with institutions generally. The breadth of research into societal ordering and institutional formation should make it clear that there is no perfect system of institutional choice. No existing institutional structure or status quo is inherently perfect as it is.

THINK ABOUT IT ...
Preview to Institutional Impact Analysis

Researchers and analysts use **institutional analysis** to break down various aspects of institutions to better understand how they change, grow and affect various aspects of our economy or our world more generally. **Institutional impact analysis** is a specific type of institutional analysis that attempts to explain how alternative institutional structures affect instances of human interdependence (conflict) and substantive economic outcomes of wealth and its distribution. What are the economic performance consequences of alternative rules? What are the non-economic performance consequences? Institutional impact analysis tackles these questions through the lens of the existing institutional structure and can be as broad or as specific as the researcher chooses. For instance, institutional impact analyses have been conducted on broad topics ranging from the regulation of airspace and payday lending, to analyzing the performance of alternative institutions for managing environmental and natural resources (Atkinson and Reed, 1990; Kaplowitz et al., 2008; Kasper, 2014).

The characteristic of note in all is that they feature a careful specification of the institutional variable. This is starkly different from other forms of impact analysis that are not concerned with institutional variables. The form of institutional impact analysis used in this book is also focused on analyzing alternative structures, rather than conducting an analysis focused on only a single institution or type of institution. This falls in line with the assumption that people – regardless of their level of rationality – consider multiple alternatives when faced with changing trade-offs or other conditions.

1.2   NORMATIVE BIAS IN ECONOMICS

Whenever we are devising strategies for handling human interdependence, we are inherently making choices involving institutions. It is therefore necessary to cultivate some understanding of institutions and how to specify the institutional variable. In the field of economics particularly, economists are often asked to evaluate or predict the outcomes or "performance" of alternate institutions. That this is often done in the absence of quality data or information in general is a testament to the challenging task economists in this position have before them. This is complicated further by the desire of most to remain scientific and logical neutral parties, reliant only on "the facts" of their analyses.

When economists attempt to do research or evaluate policy choice, they often do so under the assumption of neutrality. This approach is called **positive economics**. In introductory economics courses, positive economics is defined as objective and fact based. **Normative economics** is subjective and value based. Another way of thinking about these two concepts is that normative analyses are concerned with *what ought to be* or *what should be*, whereas positive analysis is concerned with *what is*. Generating testable hypotheses, conducting the tests and reporting the results fall in the realm of a positive economic analysis. Most comments beyond this, unless very carefully specified, fall into the realm of the normative.

This understanding of economics as either normative or positive is fairly standard, but potentially fraught. As far back as Adam Smith to as recently as John Maynard Keynes (and, indeed, many institutionalists to this day), economics has been understood as a moral science. It is only with the rise of neoclassical economics that the moral and ethical dimensions of the field have fallen to the wayside (Peil and Staveren, 2009). Milton Friedman is credited with much of this shift via his famous 1953 essay "The methodology of positive economics" (1953b), where he provides his vision of economics as a positive science. There has been some pushback and much caution against economic reductionism with regards to rationality, welfare economics and the like, including notable arguments from Nobel Laureates such as Ronald Coase and Amartya Sen.[7] The larger question is: when these analyses are so entwined with the humanly devised rules that are institutions, is neutral analysis possible?

As stated in *The Handbook of Economics and Ethics*,

> values are part of economic analysis, alongside and frequently intertwined with facts, rather than being separated from facts in the form of policy recommendations following a supposedly value-free analysis. This connection between facts and values is revealed in economic terms such as "freedom of choice," "equilibrium" and "efficiency" as being "optimal." (Peil and Staveren, 2009)

This use of language is familiar to anyone with a knowledge of economics or economic arguments of the past near century. For instance, in the heat of debate over cases like *Miller* (1928) described at the start of the chapter, we often hear some version of "let the market decide." Is this a positive or normative statement? One interpretation of "let the market decide" is that the opportunity should be sold to the highest bidder (or given to what is expected to be the highest bidder). This is hardly neutral or natural. Such a method of distributing new rights just makes them an extension of existing rights. Those that have a lot will get more. The deeper meaning of "let the market decide" is that rights should be given to those who already have many (Schmid, 2004).

In the *Miller* (1928) case, leaving things up to the market would mean that the cedar owner's right[8] to grow trees on their property now also extends to a right to poison nearby apple trees with a pathogenic pest that was previously not considered in the assignment of rights. The apple growers could do nothing, short of attempting to bargain or reason with the cedar owner. This places a previously unaccounted for or unknown burden on the apple growers. The apple owner's right to grow apple trees on their property has now been limited by their neighbor's conflicting right. By doing nothing, the burden would fall on the apple grower, where previously there was none. This kind of unmediated and undefined conflict can easily spiral out of control, often to the point where one party does something more obviously illegal. In this case, the Virginia legislature stepped in to adjust the current institutional arrangement, granting the public interest in apples more weight over the public's interest in cedar trees, a normative decision ultimately upheld by the U.S. Supreme Court.

Any form of analysis involving interactions between people and the allocation of resources for people is subject to some normative bias. This is simply the reality of working with a human variable, or an institutional variable. This means that it is the responsibility of the analyst to be clear about the implications or assumptions that accompany the starting point of an analysis, especially when working with institutional variables.

As we learned early in the chapter, institutional impact analysis is a specific type of institutional analysis that attempts to explain how alternative institutional structures affect instances of human interdependence (conflict), and substantive economic outcomes of wealth and its distribution. Think carefully about that definition. Is it truly possible to avoid using normative knowledge when analyzing wealth and its distribution? This issue of normative versus positive analysis will continue to come up throughout this text. In Chapter 2 we will use Hohfeldian legal analysis to begin to formally model structures of rights to assist the reader in conducting institutionally aware analysis.

THINK ABOUT IT …
Normative Arguments

A second interpretation of "let the market decide" involves a much more obviously normative position: party A is seen as the natural owner and if anyone else wants to have the opportunity, they must buy it. This position is well illustrated in the debate between famous institutionalists James Buchanan and Warren Samuels (1975) over *Miller* (1928). Buchanan saw the court's mediation as the heavy hand of the state destroying human freedom.

Is the institutional variable properly specified in this proposition?
As explained by Schmid (2004):

[Buchanan] proposed a market solution to the governmental regulation: Let the orchardists buy out the cedar grower if they can. If they cannot, then orchardists will have to economize as best they can. He worked with an institutional variable specification that separated the state from the distribution of ownership. It seemed natural to him that the cedar grower owned not only the land upon which the tree was growing but also the surface of neighboring apple tree leaves where the associated disease spores generated on the cedars come to rest. The physical production function for growing cedars has inputs of land, labor, and space for the spores. All of these things are necessarily consumed in the process of growing cedars.

Samuels turned Buchanan's normative reasoning on its head: There is nothing natural about who owns the opportunity to grow trees unimpeded. Rather it is a matter to be decided. In this case, as described above, the rules and laws impacting who is the owner of the various parts of apple and cedar production directly influenced who is perceived as the "natural" owner by Buchanan. But had these rules been different, so too would this status quo.

In order to conduct positive analysis of institutional impact or change, it is necessary to remember two points:

1. **"The state creation of rights is antecedent to the market, not an alternative to it**. The market just carries out the implications of ownership. The market can work with either party being the buyer or seller. But it cannot be the process by which ownership is created" (Schmid, 2004).

2. **"The conception of the state and market as alternatives is a misspecification of variables**. One can have state owned or privately owned orchards, but one cannot have a market without a state. This statement must be modified in the sense that the process of making rights (who is seller and who buyer) can be informal rather than a matter of explicit legislative or judicial choice. When new interdependencies are discovered, one party may assert ownership and, if accepted, trading begins. In this process the party that can make its interest appear more natural may become the de facto owner and in fact later be confirmed by the common law or formal statute" (Schmid, 2004).

Source: This example is taken from Schmid (2004, chapter 5.5).

1.3 TAXONOMY OF INSTITUTIONS

Institutions clearly can take many forms with many characteristics. A taxonomy must be carefully specified as one seeks to understand institutions and conduct institutional analysis. In this section, we break institutions into two groups and provide descriptions of each. We also introduce and define the nested decision-making hierarchy characteristic of institutions.

1.3.1 Formal and Informal Institutions

To conceptualize and create a common language for discussing institutions, we can break them into two general types: formal and informal (see Table 1.1). They differ primarily in the way we think about the process of their creation and their mode of enforcement.

Table 1.1   Formal versus informal institutions

Formal institutions	Informal institutions
Constrain behavior	Constrain behavior
Reliant on external enforcement	Not always reliant on external enforcement
Include written laws and regulations	Include personal habit, social conventions and
Embedded in informal institutions/norms	norms
	Influence formal institutions

Informal institutions are social norms and customs that do not always rely on external monitoring or policing of individuals' behavior. Examples of informal institutions include social conventions such as shaking hands when you meet someone, the way you might be expected to dress in any given situation or the social norm of saying "hello" when you greet someone and "goodbye" when you hang up the phone. Informal institutions include personal habits, such as the time you go to bed each night or wake up to exercise in the morning. There are also informal rules governing general social interdependence, or situations where interdependent agents are faced with choices for which individual rationality does not yield a socially optimal outcome (Voss, 2001). The prisoner's dilemma and situations involving public goods are examples.

Formal institutions are the constitutional laws and state regulations that apply to individuals, written rules within organizations and the upstream rules for how laws are made. Formal institutions typically rely on some kind of structured and well-known regulation and enforcement. These are the things that typically come to mind when you hear the word "institution." These rules of the game are the functional underpinnings of our economy, influencing who is buyer and who is seller, cost structures and every other aspect of the market.

Informal customs can become formal institutions over time. Examples of this include traditions of doing business or negotiation that eventually became part of contract law or other social norms that are eventually codified, like smoking and non-smoking rules.

The modes of enforcement present for each type of institution can also be categorized by some concept of "formalness." The external enforcement of formal institutions refers to legal consequences codified somewhere and acted upon. By contrast, more "internal" forms of enforcement might include social punishment (shaming, public censure, etc.), personal ethics or some feeling of "following the law." We will talk more about enforcement later in the text when we discuss the structural and performance pieces of the impact analysis framework.

Institutional analysis as defined in this book focuses predominantly on formal institutions, or the "rules of the game" as outlined in various levels of legal text or organizational code. Going forward, however, it is important to keep in mind both types of institutions, especially in situations where the division between formal and informal is not always clear.

1.3.2 Levels of Institutions and Analysis

Formal institutions can be broken down into two types: rules for making rules (decision rules) or rules in use. These groups look different depending on the country or region in question, but in general all rules can be thought of as fitting generally into these two categories.

To properly specify the boundaries of these groups, a few definitions are needed. First, the **law** is the system of rules which a particular country or community recognizes as regulating the actions of its members and which it may enforce by the imposition of penalties (Oxford English Dictionary, 2020a). This is distinct from a **rule**, which is one of a set of explicit or understood regulations or principles governing conduct within a particular activity or sphere (Oxford English Dictionary, 2020b). Laws are generally enforceable (and recognized), whereas rules have varying degrees of enforceability, subject to their adherence with laws or the lack of a law outlining how a particular rule can be made or enforced (common in situations pertaining to new technologies[9]). **All laws are rules, but rules are not always laws**.

Formal institutions (both laws and rules), apply to a **legal entity**, which is a lawful or legally standing association, corporation, partnership, proprietorship, trust or individual (Garner, 2019). A legal entity has the legal capacity to (1) enter into agreements or contracts, (2) assume obligations, (3) incur and pay debts, (4) sue and be sued in its own right and (5) be accountable for illegal activities (Garner, 2019). Examples of legal entities include corporations, trusts, sole proprietorships, non-profit organizations and charities, limited liability companies, as well as various other types of business forms.

Formal institutions also apply to all other going concerns, regardless of their legal status, up to a point. The **going concern** is a set of individuals with diverse preferences who function as a team to produce some kind of goods or service (tangible or otherwise). A going concern could be a family, a village or town, a private or public corporation, a nation or an international governing body or even an informal gathering of colleagues. It is based on the idea that people group together in formal and informal ways to accomplish a set of goals or objectives.[10] These groups have working rules that must be specified before moving forward.[11] The operation of any going concern will depend upon the capability of individuals to form stable expectations about the behavior of others by knowing the working rules (Ostrom, 1976). Understanding when something is a specific type of legal entity versus a going concern (and under what rules or regulation they might fall) will become important when outlining institutional structure and alternatives in the following chapters.

All laws and rules that apply to legal entities may be subject to higher-level laws that have legal **supremacy**. For instance, there is a statement in Article VI of the U.S. Constitution called the "Supremacy Clause" that states that constitutional laws are the laws of the land and all other laws are subservient to and bound by the laws laid down by the Constitution (Garner, 2019). Federal laws must adhere to constitutional laws. State laws must also. Supremacy is not always straightforward, however. For instance, whether state laws must adhere to federal laws is a question often up for debate depending on the subject matter and specificity and interpretation of the Constitution.

Supremacy is a generalizable concept that applies to most organizations, state or otherwise.[12] From a modeling perspective, supremacy simply tells us that downstream rules are conditioned by upstream rules. This is true even within private organizations, where certain rules predicate any others. For instance, many workplaces have overarching rules that state business hours where all employees must be present, often 9–3 or 8–5. Your division manager may make a rule that allows you scheduling flexibility to come in for any eight-hour period, but only if it overlaps with these mandatory hours (say, 8–4 or 9–6). Those mandatory working hours function as the rules your manager must follow when making any subsequent rules, or the rules for making rules.

Rules for how operational laws or organizational rules can be made or for who is included in lower-level decision-making processes are known as the **rules for making rules**. Rules for making rules (or laws for making laws) are everywhere. In the U.S., the highest level of rules for making rules are found in the U.S. Constitution. Constitutional institutions provide the basic rights of individuals and groups as well as the broad framework of legislative and judicial bodies. For example, at this level we decide that people may not be enslaved, there is universal suffrage, proportional representation, rights of *habeas corpus*, etc. (Schmid, 2004, p. 80). Whenever choices are made regarding a new institutional arrangement or a new set of rules, these choices themselves are made via some existing higher-level set of rules, such as some form of collective choice or constitution. **These rules for making rules form the upstream institutional context in which choices are made**.

Interdependence between people can be caused by these higher-level rules that are often held constant for analysis. When a school board or a university board moves to enact a new rule on campus, they must go through the proper channels set out in rules above them that dictate who can vote, whether the issue comes to vote, etc. These new rules in turn have implications for downstream groups and individuals, who now must adjust their decision-making processes to account for this new rule. Similarly, when the U.S. Securities and Exchange Commission (SEC) proposes new securities rules, they do so within an existing framework of laws that applies to independent agencies of the federal government. These laws can influence how effective the new SEC rules may be. This conditioning is important for the analyst to be aware of.

While the rules for making rules can be held constant for practical and analytical reasons, it is necessary for the analyst not to confuse this with implying that these rules are "natural" or "right." They simply provide the institutional context for the current issue at hand, and themselves can be subject to change at a different level of analysis.

The situation under analysis, or instance of interdependence, is a function of the actual rules in use. **Rules in use** are the everyday rules that shape how opportunities are apportioned to individuals and groups.[13] In other words, they are the rule or rules at the heart of institutional analysis. In institutional impact analysis, this is the focus for which alternatives are evaluated.

Rules in use can be separated into two categories: (1) operational laws and (2) organizational rules.

Operational laws are, quite broadly, the actual legal statutes and codes that govern our daily lives. These are set down by various federal, state and local bodies, and include everything from criminal code to state or local speeding and traffic laws. These rules may change more frequently and can provide important natural experiments for the analyst to test the potential impact of various alternatives across time and space. Firms both operate under these given laws and influence these laws as able (Schmid, 2004).

Organizational rules are not laws, but a set of rules to which members of a legal entity are required to follow. Some rules are unique to the organization and some are chosen from a set available to others. Still more are obligatory and given as a result of a larger rule-making organization or the state, or of operational laws that have supremacy. Corporations, non-profit entities and even governments themselves are structured on the basis of a set of organizational rules. These rules would be enforced using a variety of internal sanctions. For example, a firm such as Nestlé uses corporate laws given by the state (both federal and more local), but is empowered to create its own inner rules such as codes of conduct, organizational charts, contracts and alliances with others. Nestlé may also choose to enter into other agreements, such as quality certifications, labor agreements or consumer-driven certificates. These may or may not have the legal backing of the operational laws of contract law, and the level of enforcement will vary by the level of backing by operational laws that say what Nestlé may and may not do. Over time these organizational rules may form into a corporate culture with varying degrees of consciousness (Schmid, 2004).

The three levels of institutions are nested, reflecting the dynamic nature of rule making and the need for communication and interaction between the multiple actors involved. Rules in use can also be rules for making rules depending on where the analyst starts their analysis. For instance, in the Nestlé example given above, contract law (operational laws) become the rules for making rules for Nestlé's own organizational rules. While those higher-level rules may be held constant in an impact analysis of a change in those organizational rules, however, they are by no means "natural" or beyond change. They may still inform interdependence and could be brought into play in another analysis.

Figure 1.2 provides a summary to assist with analysis.

Rules for Making Rules (decision rules): Higher order institutions that create lower order institutions. Laws or rules for who is included in lower-level decision making processes or for how lower-operational laws or organizational rules can be made. Supreme. Helps structure enforcement for other levels. Ex: At a higher level: constitutions or things that function like constitutions. Rules for how certain bodies of government can formulate new laws.

At a lower level: organization-wide codes of conduct. Rules or parameters that subsequent levels of an organizational structure must make rules within.

Rules In Use: everyday rules that shape how opportunities are apportioned to individuals and groups.

---

1. **Operational Laws** (the actual **laws**): Working laws of individuals and various going concerns. Generally enforceable, but subject to supremacy. Ex: Traffic laws, voting (a constitutional law for making laws that can also be an operational law in practice).

---

2. **Organizational Rules** (internal **rules** within going concerns): Internal rules for how members of legal entities/groups relate to each other as well as rules for how members relate to other organizations or groups. Varying degrees of enforceability; subject to supremacy. ex: office rules, dress codes, rules for external communication, etc.

Figure 1.2   Levels of analysis for formal institutions

What each of these types of institutions have in common is that they all affect, or attempt to order, relationships among people. They tell individuals what they may do, what they may not do, what they must allow others to do, etc. This is all an attempt to deal with human interdependence.

1.4   HUMAN INTERDEPENDENCE

In the early twentieth century, the world became more aware of our interdependence with others around the globe than ever before. Our consumption and production choices were scrutinized for their impact on low wage workers in developing economies. There was a marked rise in environmental and natural resource conflicts. In the early twenty-first century this interdependence has only increased. We now consider our interdependence with regards to data about ourselves, our workplaces, our families and our decisions. We cannot deny that we live in a world where interdependence is ubiquitous. Untangling the relationships and the rules surrounding them only becomes more complicated with time.

At their core, institutions are the result of human interdependence. There would be no need to have a judicial system for solving disputes if individuals did not have disputes. Moreover, the fact of scarcity means that one person's actions almost always affect the welfare of another. This is interdependence. If there was unlimited access to a pest-free environment for both the cedar and the apple grower, there would be no dispute. But a pest-free environment in *Miller* (1928) is a scarce resource, one whose provision is precluded by the use of the other. Who gets what? This has to be sorted out and given order. Institutions exist to do this.

1.4.1   Interdependence as the Unit of Observation

Interdependence comes in many forms, but it is always reciprocal in nature. When a candy maker goes about his work with the help of his noisy machines, he causes a problem for the doctor next door (Coase, 1960). This scenario may sound familiar to the environmental economist or others who are familiar with the issue of externalities. The production of one firm's product imposes a cost or "externality" on those impacted by the noise generated. This is often seen as the problem to be addressed. But, as we explain here, externalities are ubiquitous. Externality is the name we give to some results of interdependence.

The key point often missed in these discussions is the mutuality or **reciprocal nature** of the problem (Coase, 1960). If the noisy machines were not there, the doctor would have peace. Yet if the doctor was not there, the machines would not be a problem. Ceasing the "harm" the candy maker is doing to the doctor would harm the candy maker (the extra expense of being quiet, whatever form that takes). Allowing it to continue harms the doctor, be it through a lack of focus resulting in lost clients or some other cost. It is selective perception to say that the candy maker harms the doctor rather than the other way around. The root of the issue is that the doctor and the candy maker are interdependent, not that there is an external effect of the machines.

When we focus on this interaction between two people and the reciprocal nature of the problem, we can more easily perceive what is traded on the market as being less about physical things and more about the rights that individuals possess to perform certain actions, as established by the legal system (Coase, 1992). A situation of interdependence is both predicated on existing rules and perpetuated by the messy ways in which humans interact with them. The candy maker might be perceived as having a "right" to utilize their space in any way they see fit, but if the doctor is said to have the same right, where do we go next? We could say that their respective leases might include or should include some clarification as to how either can reasonably expect to use the space (i.e. some stipulation about "unreasonable noise," etc.), but that is now clarifying the issue by affording the doctor a "right" that he did not clearly have before. Moreover, the ramifications of the doctor's quiet or his candy-making neighbor's noise can only be thought of as externalities if each of them cares little for the impact their actions have on others. If painting a more complete picture, it is just another cost.

Think about a situation where the downstairs neighbor in your apartment complex uses an alarm that makes a repetitive and jarring noise of a rooster crowing. Due to the positioning of the units' bedrooms, this alarm has the unpleasant effect of also waking you up every morning. What can be done here? You might argue that you have the right to sleep until whatever time you wish undisturbed, but the downstairs neighbor could easily argue that the use of an alarm clock in their own home is their own right.[14] Unless there is some highly specific language about the use of alarm clocks in your lease, or some guarantee on the part of the apartment complex to afford you a certain level of quiet at the time in question, the respective rights between you and your neighbor are a matter to be sorted out.

Again, interdependence is ubiquitous. It is never possible for us to do "just one thing." You might decide on an informal, workable solution between you and your neighbor that clarifies your conflict somewhat, but you will remain interdependent. Even if the apartment management should side with you after you lodge a formal complaint, and the offending alarm is banned, you and your neighbor remain interdependent. Negotiation is a mediation of the interdependence here, but it does not end it. It simply modifies its current state.

Much of the institutional economics literature has been based on the idea of transactions between parties. In transactions with each other we can understand how the rules of the game shape the outcome of the transaction. The word "transaction" infers to most people an idea of entering into a voluntary and likely situation of bargaining between parties. However, this conception fails to fully engage the idea of interdependence. Interdependence takes on the idea that we and our decisions are interconnected even if we have not entered into a bargaining situation. This reciprocal nature of human interaction, or interdependence, is the focus of our discussion and analysis of institutions. Our unit of observation going forward is the **situation of interdependence**. No model can be properly specified without an understanding of the existing structure and parties involved, and a focus on interdependence best captures this.

There are many examples of interdependence in the economic realm. Some of these interdependencies are based on the biological or physical characteristics of the world we inhabit and some of the interdependencies are based on how we as humanity structure our lives. Sometimes the interdependence is between two agents and sometimes between multiple agents at the same time.

The tools in this book are designed to describe and examine situations of interdependence between economic agents. The simplest way to start this analysis is by determining who is dependent on whom or, in other words, how the actions and behavior of one group of economic agents impact other agents and vice versa. If we identify a situation of this type where mutual interaction and interdependence exist, the tools in this text can help clarify, investigate and examine such situations. This interdependence exists in traditional economic relationships such as between an employer and employee, consumers and retailers, manufacturers and wholesalers, but also in any scenario where one economic agent's actions, whether intentional or not, have implications for other agents.

The point of view expressed in this book is that all forms of internal and external effects are part of the broader conception of interdependence.[15] Externalities of all forms are ubiquitous in the economy. Therefore, interdependence is the starting point and the unit of observation for our approach. Rather than name it an externality or just market interaction, we focus on board conception of interdependence or how decisions made by one set of economics agents impacts another and how institutions structure that interdependence.

THINK ABOUT IT …
Interdependence and Opportunity Sets

Air space is just as much a physical input in the production function of candy as are labor, sugar and machines. Likewise, air space is as much a physical input into the production function for medical services as are labor and medicine. The unavoidable institutional issue is in whose opportunity set is the scarce commodity. If there is to be a market for this opportunity, the issue is who is the buyer and who is the seller. Whoever is made the owner, they will listen to the bids and pleas of the non-owner. If the bid is insufficient, the non-owner suffers. That someone suffers from scarcity is inevitable. This suffering cannot be remedied by any institutional cleverness whether tax, regulation or market. These just make manifest the underlying rule-created opportunity set distribution.

Source: Schmid (2004, 72).

1.4.2 Describing Interdependence as Physical or Biological Characteristics

In some cases, interdependence can be thought of as based on the physical or biological characteristics of the tangible or intangible economic goods in question. Schmid developed a classification system based on what he called the "inherent characteristics of the good in question." Economic conflict, or interdependence, he argued, could all be traced back to these six characteristics of economic "goods."[16] Through them, we might begin to understand the institutional issues that are leading to interdependence. We discuss these good types more in Chapter 3.

Characteristics highlighted by Schmid include the degree of incompatibility (scarcity and/or rivalry), exclusion cost, economies of scale, the effect of another user on cost, the cost to produce another physical unit and various information and transaction costs (Schmid, 2004, 16, 90). Schmid's good types extend to goods or services that have multiple characteristics, depending on the particular case of interdependence being analyzed. Vaccines, for instance, have many characteristics:

- high exclusion cost good (disease protection) between vaccinated person A and unvaccinated person B;
- high information cost good (if you think the vaccine could be dangerous) between unvaccinated person B and the drug manufacturer that they do not trust; and
- economies of scale good (high upfront research and development costs, each marginal user less costly).[17]

Depending on the specific situation or problem at hand, the key characteristic(s) could be identified, and the conflict addressed in some way if the challenges of the particular good type were addressed. But your method for describing or identifying interdependence need not rely on this broad list. Good types are just one tool for getting to the heart of interdependence. A vocabulary for breaking conflict into legal-type relationships might be all that is necessary. Use whatever tools or training you have at your disposal to begin thinking about the interdependence and where it's coming from. These tools, when combined with the basic legal framework introduced in Chapter 2, provide a great starting point for describing and understanding the institutional situation – the first piece of institutional impact analysis. More information on these concepts will be introduced in Chapter 3.

1.5   CHAPTER RECAP

- The word **institution** has been used in many different ways in the economics literature. For our purposes, we define institutions as "**sets of ordered relationships among people that define their rights, their exposure to the rights of others, their privileges, and their responsibilities**" (Schmid, 2004). Broken down, this simply means that institutions are the rules that structure interaction between people. These rules outline what we can, cannot, may and may not do and they apply in a correlative fashion to all parties in any given socio-economic interaction. With this definition, we can begin to analyze and understand how to apply the concept of "institution" in an analytical fashion and determine the likely performance of the given situation. This is the driving factor behind the development of a formal model of institutional analysis.

- **Institutional analysis** is designed to help us deconstruct the world around us and propose an understanding of the connection between people, the rules of the game and economic performance. As we learned early in the chapter, **institutional impact analysis** is a specific type of institutional analysis that attempts to explain how alternative institutional structures affect instances of human interdependence (conflict) and substantive economic outcomes of wealth and its distribution.
- **Formal institutions** can be broken down into **rules for making rules** and **rules in use**. These apply to all **going concerns** and **legal entities**.
- While working with an institutional variable, it is important to be aware of knowledge that is **normative** in nature versus knowledge that is **positive** in nature, and be clear about the possible implication of assumptions or the starting point of the analysis.
- Efficiency is a normative concept that is based on measures of economic performance (prices, quantity produced, etc.) under one set of rules (institutions) and/or versus another.
- Institutional impact analysis starts with understanding the nature of the **interdependence** between the parties. Interdependence is simply the fact that parties can take actions and those actions will impact, positively and negatively, the reality facing the other parties in the situation. Interdependence may come from physical and biological characteristics of the situation and the goods and services involved or from the nature of the institutions (rules) currently in place. The **Situation of Independence** is our Unit of Observation going forward

NOTES

1. See Samuels (1972), Buchanan (1972) and Buchanan and Samuels (1975).
2. Several economists have described the market as having a natural existence then reigned in, or modified, by individuals, if the market will bear it. Williamson, for instance, famously proposed that "in the beginning there were markets" (Williamson, 1975, p. 20).
3. To remain in form with the Hohfeld framework of jural relations (introduced in Chapter 2), Schmid's definition might be better reimagined as "Institutions are sets of ordered relationships among people that define their legal entitlements and disablements." Since this is not what he wrote, however, and given the minute difference, we utilize the original as used in Schmid (2004).

4. We are being somewhat vague with language here. Socially enforceable simply means that there is some general understanding and acceptance of one's claim, whether or not it is enforced. In Chapter 2, we define a Hohfeldian right, which is always paired with a subsequent duty, and is different from the very general use of the word "rights."
5. See also North (1994) for more discussion of the importance of ideologies and cognitive classifications as well as the limits of the rational choice framework.
6. Herbert Simon (1955), who built much of his work around the importance of realism of assumptions, gave credit to early institutional economics (such as the work of John R. Commons) as foundational to behavioral economics.
7. See such articles as Coase (1982) and Sen (1987, 1992, 1997).
8. In this case, the 'right' is actually a Hohfeldian Privelege, but we will get to that in Chapter 2.
9. Consider the "net neutrality" debate, the regulation of "gig" workers and contractors, especially with the growth of telework.
10. In grouping together going concerns formulate, again formally or informally, a set of rules or institutions that will guide the group's conduct. Human society, especially in the modern age, is full of millions of informal and formal going concerns (Simon, 1955). When conflict arises in the group, the group resolves that conflict through whatever mechanism they have in place or develop, and a new set of institutions or rules emerges out of conflict to guide the group.
11. The working rules term is used rather than "legal" because the rules can be expressed for any going concern not just the formal government entity of that jurisdiction.
12. Similar concepts also exist in other legal systems, though the Supremacy Clause and legal system as discussed here is Anglo-American specific.
13. Bromley (1989, p. 49) refers to everyday rules such as these as governing "commodity transactions." Everyday rules are how opportunities are apportioned to individuals and groups by alternative formal property rights in the context of given habits/customs and given technology.
14. More specifically, this would likely be considered a Hohfeldian "privilege." More on that in Chapter 2.
15. Why the emphasis on interdependence? Isn't economics already about the interdependence between buyers and sellers? Economists do study the market interactions between buyers and sellers and they discuss the unintentional interactions of economic agents called externalities or external effects. Externalities are discussed as being of a form known as technological externalities and pecuniary externalities. Technological externalities, like the situation of a polluting firm, were considered potential market failures and could be addressed by government policy. Pecuniary externalities were those that resulted from "in-market" interactions and not market failures. For example, if a competing business opens that harms your business, this would be a form of a pecuniary externality and not a market failure.
16. Schmid used "goods" non-traditionally, and later included services and other intangibles under the umbrella of good types.
17. Taking this even further, the argument could be made that vaccines are actually a network good, a subset of economies of scale, since more users means increased benefit for everyone.

2. The underlying legal structure of economic relationships

To have an opportunity in your opportunity set is to have power. To alter institutions is to alter power, and if it makes a difference in performance, there is a measure of power. (Schweikhardt, 2016)

Recall from Chapter 1 our discussion of the Cedar Rust Act and Miller et al. v. Schoene *(1928), a situation highlighting several instances of interdependence including that between apple orchardists and cedar owners (Miller), as well as the state entomologist (Schoene), who carried out the ruling of the Virginia courts when he ordered the removal of cedar trees on Miller's property without compensation. In the Cedar Rust case the Virginia courts ultimately passed and later upheld the Cedar Rust Act, finding that, "There is no taking when the government destroys one type of property to protect another type of property that the government has identified as having greater value to the public."*

But what does this ruling really mean? How can we, as economic analysts, begin to analyze this case so we might be able to carefully answer economic or social questions arising from it? How might we begin to conduct an impact analysis of this decision?

To understand institutional structure in a particular situation, we begin with a discussion of the many legal relations in the case. Like many academics who have commented on *Miller* (1928) in the years since, we are interested in the integral change in the distribution of "rights" (a term used loosely here) that occurred between the involved parties. But what is a right? And what does it say about "rights" that they can be so easily changed or taken from one person and given to another, as was seemingly done in this case? Didn't the cedar owners have just as much of a right to grow their trees as the apple growers had to grow theirs? How can one right be favored over the other? These are the questions to be explored.

Institutional structure is partly composed of the legal structure of any jurisdiction, including those higher-level rules-for-making rules (be it operational laws or organizational rules) that structure the alternative rules-in-use available, and the rules-in-use themselves. These rules form the upstream institutional context in which choices are made. For instance, consider that businesses are organized based on state laws – these laws allow for certain types of investment structures, and also provide background 'rules for making rules' related to the election and voting of the board of directors, for example.

The *Miller* (1928) case and others like it are inherently about a murky institutional structure, one that did not previously conceive of the issue of cedar rust, but that has been tasked with addressing it all the same.

Think about other situations where the existing structure or rules in use were seemingly unprepared for some change. The 2020 pandemic is one obvious recent example. Choices were made at every level that involved some previously undefined weighing of whose health and safety – or whose right to continue business as usual – mattered, and to what degree. Through sorting these things out, decision makers were able to move forward. Institutional structure was changed in some way, and changed again, as institutions struggled to respond to unprecedented situations. In the case of COVID-19 in the U.S., many institutions were primed for change yet again as a new administration took office in the midst of the pandemic. As legal disputes emerge in subsequent years, still more will need to be sorted out.

In this chapter, we introduce an analytical framework for understanding and discussing institutional structure. We adopt a language of legal relations developed by legal scholar Wesley Hohfeld in the 1910s and we acknowledge a few modifications by economics scholar John R. Commons in the 1920s. The Hohfeldian legal framework as used here will provide a toolkit for describing, in set terms, interdependence and the institutional variable at work in a specific situation. This same toolkit will enable readers to conceive of available structural alternatives more clearly. This is applied to a model of institutional impact analysis in Chapter 3.

By the end of this chapter, you should be able to specify the institutional variable and its structure(s). You will be able to:

1. Use the Hohfeldian framework to describe the legal (institutional) framework in an economic situation.
2. Define who has the right and who has the duty in a particular situation and how they relate to one another.
3. Assess the legal power and immunities of economic agents as they seek to transact.
4. Tie various legal (institutional) positions to economic stocks and flows for various agents.

2.1   DEFINING INSTITUTIONAL STRUCTURE

The economic analyst needs a toolkit or language to frame the institutional or legal relations underlying the transactions that are occurring in the economy and the general level of interdependence between various agents in the economy. Schmid (2004) wrote:

> A full understanding of institutions must include informal, tacit, and internalized rights as well as those formal relationships legislated and sanctioned by the state. Institutions are more than the rules of the game providing constraints. They are also enablement to do what the individual cannot do alone. They also affect beliefs and preferences, and provide cues to uncalculated action.

Here we primarily focus on providing descriptors for the formal relationships that guide or structure our interdependence with others. Most economic analysis begins with identifying a set of buyers and sellers and some other basic characteristics of a market or exchange setting such as the total volume in the market, possibly characteristics of the goods from a consumption and production point of view and other such factors. However, all transactions are occurring with a background of legal relations existing between buyers and sellers or other parties in the economy. It is partly this legal framework that informs the nature of interdependence between transacting parties, whether it is the Uniform Commercial Code, common law, statutory law, constitutional law or even international law. These are important in determining who is the buyer and seller and who has what to trade.

Too often, the legal and institutional background and framework is neglected (Schmid, 1999). This chapter provides economic analysts with a new language to uncover that institutional background. This language will cause the analyst to ask some basic questions about the rights and duties of the various interdependent parties and how the current and proposed changes to that institutional structure will drive economic performance and distributional outcomes. These background conditions are essential before buyers and sellers get to the business of transacting, or indeed interacting in general.

Let us start with a general scenario.

Example 2.1: Public accommodation
Recently, there has been great debate regarding the ability of a retailer to provide a good or service to a client. Some retailers, for religious or other personal reasons, have decided that they do not wish to provide their goods or service to a client based on the characteristics or lifestyle decisions of that client. Many states in the U.S. have what are called "public accommodation laws." These laws prohibit the discrimination by a "public accommodation" enterprise against individual consumers based on a number of potential characteristics such as race, gender, marital status and religion. A "public accommodation" is generally considered a commercial enterprise that is open to non-employees.

In those states that have a public accommodation law, the rules are generally that the retailer must open the business to customers without discrimination to various characteristics as specified in the rules. These rules clearly restrict the decision-making space that is open to retailers who remain open to the public at large. This type of regulation may not impose a direct cost on a retailer such as a rule that requires a business license to operate in that community, but it nevertheless shapes the decision-making sphere of the retailer.

In a state that has a public accommodation rule (AR), the retailer faces a duty or obligation to serve customers who meet certain characteristics without discrimination. The customers who meet these criteria have the legal power to enter a commercial establishment and be provided the goods or service from the retailer (assuming they have the ability to pay). This expands the opportunity set for the customers relative to the retailers.

In contrast, there are some U.S. states that do not have public accommodation laws (NR). In those states, it may be the case that under the rule (NR), customers with certain characteristics will be excluded from buying from certain sellers. Their market options are therefore restricted, and they may perhaps face higher prices or other costs as compared to customers in states that have public accommodation laws (AR) and more options.

Famously, the economist and Nobel Prize winner Milton Friedman argued that free markets would eliminate racism and other forms of discrimination. His argument was that sellers who discriminated would be driven out by sellers who did not discriminate. Friedman's argument included the idea that anti-discrimination laws were unnecessary and imposed coercion. As he wrote, "But in a society based on free discussion, the appropriate recourse is for me to seek to persuade them that their tastes are bad and that they should change their views and their behavior, not to use coercive power to enforce my tastes and my attitudes on others" (Freidman, 1962). Once we apply the interdependence model as expressed by legal scholar Wesley Hohfeld, however, the question of coercion becomes one of a dual-sided nature.

Coercion can be defined as the imposition of **an obligation or the withdrawal of an option or opportunity on an economic agent**. The problem with Freidman's story is that coercion works in both directions. The commercial enterprises and their owners are obligated (or in some minds, coerced) in an anti-discrimination legal environment. On the other hand, this same legal environment expands rights and choice sets of buyers, especially buyers who have the protected characteristics. A legal environment that does not have anti-discrimination laws in regards to public accommodations results in a shift in the rights and obligations in the opposite direction. Each of these legal or institutional environments results in a different distribution of economic performance. The Hohfeldian framework provides the economic analyst with a language to describe the legal and institutional environment and understand the various differences of how the dynamics will play out in each situation.

2.2 THE HOHFELDIAN LEGAL FRAMEWORK

In Chapter 1, we introduced institutions as sets of ordered relationships among people that define their rights, their exposure to the rights of others, their privileges and their responsibilities (Schmid, 2004) and explored how they define and constrain opportunity sets. Expanding on this, the institutional structure (legal structure) is the system through which parties act, cooperate, conflict with and interact with one another. Legal theory can provide new insight into economic relations and performance. When viewed through the lens of formal institutional structures, this can be thought of as a series of legal relations action verbs expressed as rights and duties in establishing the relationship of the parties to one another.[1]

But why should it matter? One important concept in economics, the so-called Coase Theorem, states that under a certain set of assumptions the law is essentially irrelevant to the economic performance and outcomes.[2] The structure of the law and who has what rights, duties and obligations should not matter as the parties will transact to reach the optimum or efficient level of distribution of economic resources in any case. However, a crucial assumption in the Coase Theorem is that of zero transaction costs.

Transaction costs are clearly an ever present phenomenon in the real world of our economy. The law and the establishment of legal rights and duties have a real impact on economic performance and distribution. They help determine who has access to goods and services, who has information or higher information costs and who has opportunities in general. There is no world of zero transaction costs. As Coase himself said in an interview in 2012, "I never liked the Coase Theorem ... I don't like it because it's a proposition about a system in which there were no transaction costs. It's a system which couldn't exist. And therefore it's quite unimaginable" (Roberts, 2012).

Yale Legal scholar Wesley N. Hohfeld provided a legal model that, used in this context, provides a language for the relations of various parties in an economic context.[3] Hohfeld's basic observation was that certain words of critical importance to the legal profession, such as the word "right," had no agreed-upon or clear meaning. Throughout his seminal work, "Some fundamental legal conceptions as applied in judicial reasoning" (1913), Hohfeld uses several examples of ownership to break down complex legal relations into their fundamental building blocks. In a dedicated effort to lend clarity to all forms of legal analysis going forward, Hohfeld developed a set of conceptions to define legal relations among parties. Rather than providing specific definitions for each of these relations, he offered three rules that each legal relation must meet:

1.   Each relation has its unique correlative (each conception is another way of stating its correlative).
2.   Each relation has its unique opposite (opposites cannot be accorded to the same party for the same act).
3.   Each relation is *never* any of the others (holding parties and acts constant).

With these three rules, Hohfeld pared things down to four legal relations that enabled him and later analysts to distinguish clearly between legal and non-legal relations (Schlag, 2015). John R. Commons of the University of Wisconsin Economics Department then added and adjusted some of Hohfeld's jural model to make it better suited for the field of economics with a more behavioral rather than logical perspective.[4] Commons followed Hohfeld in recognizing the adversarial nature of legal rights and in arguing that legal rights are, fundamentally, social relations: a myriad of legally constituted relations between individuals underwritten by the state (Fiorito, 2010, p. 269; Schmid, 2004). This stood counter to the old conception of ownership and private property which focused more closely on non-social relationships between individuals and goods, rather than from the vantage point of how ownership affects relationships among individuals and between individuals and the state.

The subsequent analytical framework is referred to as the Hohfeldian framework. This framework relies on a conception of jural correlatives, or a language for further describing four key formal relationships between parties, each pair consisting of one entitlement and a coinciding disablement. This formal language becomes crucial when conducting any kind of analysis involving interdependence, where many keywords are used in ways that are unclear.

The basic Hohfeldian framework consists of four pairs of jural correlatives: right/duties, privilege/exposure, power/liability and immunity/disability. These four relationships are both universal and irreducible (Hohfeld, 1913, p. 58, supra note 1), and include one entitlement (left) and one disablement (right). Table 2.1 lays these out.

Each jural relation is best described in terms of the agents impacted. Imagine you have two agents: Alpha and Beta. Agent Alpha has a privilege to act in a certain manner or use a specific tangible item in a certain manner. The privilege means Alpha has the ability to do something or use an item. At the same time, agent Beta is subject to potential damages without legal remedy from agent Alpha's actions. However, agent Beta may have the privilege to act in their own fashion while being exposed to agent Alpha's actions. There we flip and now party Alpha is exposed to the privilege of agent Beta to take action

Table 2.1   Jural correlatives

Entitlements	Disablements
Right: A claim that Beta must do or not do something in relation to Alpha.	Duty: The other end of a right. An obligation that Beta must do or not do something in relation to Alpha.
Privilege: Ability of Alpha to act in a certain manner without being held liable for damages to others (Beta(s)).	Exposure: Beta is subject to damages from Alpha's actions without legal remedy.
Power: Alpha's ability to change their legal relationship with Beta.	Liability: Beta's relationship to Alpha is susceptible to being changed.
Immunity: Beta's relations to Alpha cannot be legally altered by Alpha.	Disability: Alpha is unable to change their legal relationship with Beta.

or use something. The point of this example is that each agent (could be two or many more depending on the situation) must be considered from their own legal perspective as well as in relation to the other agents.

Key to this discussion of jural correlatives is that there is *always* a person (or other parties/agents including possibly the entire world) on each end. Each relation has its *unique correlative* that is a different way of talking about the same legal relation. The four entitlements on the left each coincide with a disablement on the right. If Alpha has a right that Beta must do (or not do) something, Beta has a duty to do some action (or not do action). In this manner a right is also a duty, but from the other's perspective. The other three legal relationships can be described similarly. This highlights the issue of interdependence at the heart of human conflict and cooperation. We discuss each of these relations in more detail in the following sections.

Each jural position can also be viewed as having its unique opposite. Jural opposites cannot exist for the same person or agent at the same time. If you identify an agent as having a specific Hohfeldian position, then that party cannot also be in the opposite position. The jural opposites have nothing to do with the other agents but simply are about what positions in the Hohfeldian system are incompatible for the same party.

For example, a person cannot have a right and an exposure at the same time for the same issue or concern. A person with a right has a set of formal legal relations relative to others and is not exposed to damages from that other party in a legal setting. The person with the exposure is subject to the actions of the other party with the right. These dualities as opposites move together. For instance, Alpha's exposure to negative language ends where their right to not be defamed begins.

A second set of opposites is that of duty and privilege. An agent with a duty cannot at the same time have the privilege in a relationship of a specific transactional setting. The party with a duty must do something and the party with a privilege has the freedom to act or not act.

In the power/disability pairing, the power position means that an agent has the specific ability to act, or not, in a certain way towards another party. The disability is that an agent is exposed to the actions of the opposite party. An agent has either a power to act and change legal relations or they do not and are potentially exposed.

The final opposite relationship is liability and immunity and (once again) one cannot be in both positions at once. A party with an immunity is not subject to the actions or damages being imposed by another party. The liability position means that a party is subject to the actions and damages of another party.

Analysis of a situation of interdependence should first consider the jural correlatives and opposites distinction. Remembering that each position must also reflect a correlated position, we consider how the working rules reflect the current status of the agents. Like in the public accommodation case introduced at the start of the chapter, the analyst must also remember that the existence of a right may be very specific and not reflective of the entire situation.

THINK ABOUT IT ...
Definition of Rights

In the following sections, we explain how a right to property really has more to do with someone else's duty not to trespass, and that a right without an accompanying duty (or obligation to others) is not really a right at all, but rather a privilege that others are exposed to. We will talk about how the ability to modify these legal relationships is what gives a party power, and that this power has limits, in the form of varying types of disability, immunity and liability. Once the reader has a firm grasp of these concepts, defining institutions and changes within them becomes a much less daunting task.

Consider the following statements regarding rights:

1. A party to a binding contract has a right to the other party's performance per that contract.
2. A person has a right to burn a flag.
3. The state of Michigan (where I live) has a right to call me to jury duty.
4. I have a right not to be called to jury duty in Ohio.

In these statements, the word "right" is used in four different ways. Can you create a clear, specific definition of the word right, using these four examples?

In the first, a right is a legal relationship where B must do something for A. In the second, a right is something A can do without interference from party B or C, etc. In the third example, a right is the ability of A to change interdependence with B (B is not required to do anything until called for duty) and in the fourth example, a right is just a statement of non-interdependence between A and B. The word "right" means different things in each of these examples, and only the broadest of definitions can encompass each. The Hohfeldian framework helps remedy this lack of clarity.

2.2.1 Rights and Duties

The first position in the Hohfeldian system is the right-duty relationship. A right for agent Alpha only exists in relationship or correlation to a duty that is imposed on one or more other agent Beta(s).

Rights are a claim by one agent to have another agent(s) do or not do something. A right means that another agent(s) must or must not do something; it has little to do with what the right holder can or cannot do. Although we tend to think of rights as concepts such as the "right to free speech," rights can be conceived of more generally as any claim an agent Alpha has against agent(s) Beta or any other agent that is part of the same community or society.

A right can be conceived of as part of the ongoing function of any going concern, not just related to government or legal entities. An individual agent may have a right as a member of any organizational entity including a church, community group, municipality, national government, family or household. For example, agent Alpha may have a right as a member of a church to receive certain services, and a church official may be under a duty to provide that service. There may also be a judicial-type body in that religious organization that adjudicates such disputes over rights and duties.

How does a right translate into economic terms? A right can act as both a stock and flow in economic terms. In stock terms, a right is essentially acting as an existing or contingent asset to an agent. A physical good or piece of land for example partially gains economic value because of a legal right to exclude others from use or availability. Historically, an asset in accounting terminology was defined as "rights of ownership or objects that could be exchanged for cash" (Williams, 2003). Over time, the concept of an asset expanded to become more like "service potential" or "future economic benefits." These more modern concepts of an asset are now embedded in international accounting regulations. Thus, we can observe that to hold a right provides some form of a current and future economic benefit to an agent.

In flow terms, this same right may also translate into an income stream due to other agents having to do something. People who want to use the capital or land that agent Alpha owns will be required to pay for that right thus creating an income stream for the agent. Other factors would play as well into the value of that transaction such as demand for the services of the land and land location. While these other factors may be important, agent Alpha's legal right is what establishes the baseline for any value that can be attributed to that specific individual. If agent Beta owns the right to the land, a different economic outcome or performance would then occur.

Duties are the correlative of a right. A duty means an agent Beta must perform or not perform some action or activity relative to agent Alpha who holds a right. Agent Beta may refer to one person or to multiple persons. For example, agent Alpha's right to exclude others from their property applies and creates a duty to all other persons (all potential agents Beta). A duty could also be the provision that agent Beta is in a legal relationship with agent Alpha who must do something such as make a payment or perform a certain service.

How does a duty translate into economic terms? In one sense, a duty may be regarded as an opportunity cost that must be incurred by agent Beta in regards to agent Alpha. Agent Beta, who has a duty, is required to do or not do some activity which means there is a positive or negative cost involved in doing or not doing something. A positive duty is an obligation that would therefore appear as a cost or liability in an accounting sense on the balance sheet or profit-loss statement of an individual or a going concern. A negative duty is still a reduction in agent Beta's opportunities to act. They have fewer options available to them. This may not show up on a financial balance sheet or cash flow statement but nonetheless influences the economic agent's choices.

If the analyst identifies a right, the next step then is to identify which party or parties have a duty and the type of duty. The duty could be a negative one of an act that should not occur or a positive duty that another party Gamma has an action that must take place. For example, if agent Alpha owns a parcel of property, the law likely imposes some duties on agent Beta regarding that ownership. The duty may be one of no trespassing on the property. In this case, agent Beta is under a duty not to physically enter a specific geographic space without the permission of agent Alpha. Further, this determination of ownership of a parcel of property by agent Alpha is a source of wealth and income and a potential cost of agent Beta.

Economists traditionally think a great deal about market exchanges. Given the initial distribution of rights and duties, market exchange can be thought of as the transfer of rights and duties for a certain price. Agent Alpha may be a farmer who owns several acres of land. Agent Beta may be a windmill company that wishes to lease part of the property from the farmer for a new windmill installation. If the farmer agrees, the parties trade property rights on the market. Under the contract agreed to by the parties, the farmer may now have a duty not to interfere with the windmill operation as long as the contract is in place. There has been a partial switch of rights and duties between the parties. This does not mean that the farmer has given up all rights to their property, even the leased portion, just that a piece of the right-duty correlative has shifted.

In some cases, the parties exchanging goods and services disagree about the performance of the exchange. A second-level analysis may be needed in these cases. The failure to act or not act on a duty under an exchange would lead to the creation of a potential remedy by agent Beta. If agent Alpha failed to deliver in an exchange setting as established under a contract, agent Beta may wish to sue or seek other forms of adjudication to recover from damages. We discuss legal remedies in Chapter 3.

Example 2.2 walks through a common situation where understanding the right/duty relationship can come in handy.

Example 2.2

Think about a standard lease agreement. Suppose you have a friend from another country visiting for several weeks, and you want them to stay with you. What aspects of your legal relationship with your landlord might you have to consider? There are many statements that detail what you (the tenant/ leasee) and the landlord (lessor) may or may not do with regards to tenancy of the property. Only a few likely pertain to this particular situation. Let us look at one common line in many rental agreements:

> No guests of the leasee shall occupy the premises for longer than one week without the prior written consent of the landlord.

Once you signed the lease, you have a duty to obtain written consent for any guests staying longer than one week before they surpass that amount of time. The landlord has the right that you obtain written consent or refrain from having a guest for longer than a week. If you do not do this, the landlord then has the ability to take legal action against you (or not), per the specifics of the contract and the laws of the area.

This is an example of a Hohfeldian jural relation – you have a disablement (that you must obtain consent before doing X) and your landlord has an entitlement (that you must obtain consent before you do X). A Hohfeldian jural relation is always a relation between two parties with regard to a specific act X.

Now, you may decide in this situation to simply have your friend stay and ignore any potential requirement of written consent from your landlord for various reasons. This decision or possible choice does not change the existing legal relationship. It is an issue of enforcement and legal remedy, a second level of Hohfeldian analysis introduced in the advanced topics of Chapter 3. When conducting analysis of institutional structure, it is important to separate base Hohfeldian relations from their second-tier enforcement, which can modify their meaning.

2.2.2   Privilege and Exposure

A second set of primary legal positions is the privilege-exposure relationship. **Privilege** is a legal or jural position that the holder is able to act or not in a certain manner. Notice that a simple privilege is a one-sided affair meaning an agent may act or not act, but not both. In Chapter 3, we introduce more complex forms of privilege. Privilege refers to the acts that a privilege holder can do or not do as opposed to a right where the reference point is what others must do or not do (duty).

For example, agent Alpha may have the legal privilege to start a new business. Agent Beta, who has an existing nearby business in the same field, has an exposure and is subject to damages in a legal sense without a potential remedy from the competition from agent Alpha. The legal holding of privilege creates a sphere of action or no action that can have financial value. The option to do something, or even to not do something, means that the agent's opportunity set is larger than it would be otherwise.

The holding of a privilege versus a right (or more complicated forms of privilege as described in Chapter 3) by agent Alpha may have important implications for financial and economic performance. If agent Alpha holds a right, there is more security of expectations regarding what other agents (Beta) must or must not do. While not perfect, a right holder has some level of expectation and can act accordingly. If agent Alpha only holds a privilege, they can act, but others who are exposed are not under a duty to not use their own privilege to act. Therefore, agent Alpha's security of expectations is lessened.

The analyst can also consider a situation where conditions dictate a jural change or movement from duty to privilege or right to exposure. At some point a duty ends for agent Beta, at which point they may move to a position of privilege. With a legal privilege, agent Beta is no longer required to do or not do something (as with a duty). Agent Beta may now act and even cause economic damage to agent Alpha without potentially being concerned about creating an injury with a legal remedy. In the same vein, rights are not absolute and at some point the rights of agent Alpha end. The point where a right ends means agent Alpha moves into a potentially exposed position (exposure) with respect to the privilege of agent Beta to act.

Consider again a situation where agent Beta wishes to start a competing business. Agent Beta had previously worked for agent Alpha and in so doing signed a non-compete clause. This clause had a provision that agent Beta would not leave and start a competing business in the same region for five years. After five years under this contract, agent Beta moves from a position of Hohfeldian duty into a position of Hohfeldian privilege to start a business and even cause economic damage to agent Beta. At this point, agent Alpha no longer has a Hohfeldian right that Beta not compete against their business and moves into a position of Hohfeldian exposure. Of course, this does not stop from agent Alpha responding to the actions of agent Beta.

However, simultaneously, agent Beta potentially holds a separate and distinct legal privilege relative to agent Alpha to react and respond to agent Alpha's business start-up. Agent Beta's opportunity set, in this example, is similar to agent Alpha's. The existence of a privilege for agent Alpha says nothing about Beta's potential legal privileges. Agent Beta, for example, may restructure their business, increase marketing or change their product line in response to agent Alpha's business plan.

In the case of both legal privilege and exposure, the analyst can consider each as (1) a starting point for analysis in defining who has which and (2) understanding the dynamics or changes in a situation which may move agents from positions of rights-exposures and duty-priveleges. These shifts can be caused by both private and public actions. Each legal position must be carefully and narrowly defined for each agent. In any given situation, an agent may hold a right and a privilege and also be under a duty depending on certain conditions or events occurring. Later we will see that the different legal positions may need to be combined or differentiated from one another in more complex compound formulas.

THINK ABOUT IT ...
Right-Duty and Privilege-Exposure Connection

There is a direct connection between the primary legal relations of right-duty and privilege-exposure. If we imagine a situation of a right for agent Alpha and a duty for agent Beta, at some point this relationship ends. When the right ends for agent Alpha, agent Beta is released from having a duty and vice versa. When this right-duty relationship ends, we enter into the privilege-exposure relationship. This is visually illustrated in Figure 2.1.

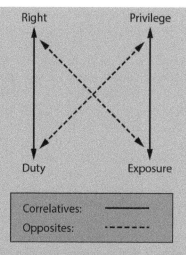

Figure 2.1   Right-duty and privilege-exposure connection

From agent Beta's perspective, the termination of duty creates a privilege to act or refrain from acting. The end of a right for agent Alpha means they are now exposed to the implications from the actions of agent Beta. The word implications is used because an exposure is not necessarily negative.

Why does this matter? The presence of a privilege versus a duty can play an important role in the financial status of an agent. A duty essentially imposes a constraint on the available actions of an agent and may imply a direct cost on an action that must occur, depending on the nature of the duty. The switch of agent Beta's position from a duty to a privilege essentially reduces a constraint and expands the opportunity set of agent Beta.

When this occurs, agent Beta gains a privilege and a release from the duty imposed and agent Alpha is now under an exposure to the actions of agent Beta. A Hohfeldian privilege is specific. Agent Beta may have a privilege to undertake an activity; that does not imply that agent Alpha cannot do activity Z. Agent Alpha may simultaneously be under a duty not to do Z. The establishment that Beta has a privilege and Alpha is exposed to the actions of Beta implies nothing about Alpha's situation in regards to what actions they can or cannot take in regards to Beta. A second analysis needs to be undertaken to determine if agent Alpha has a duty not to interfere with agent Beta or if in fact agent Alpha is privileged to act relative to agent Beta in response. The analyst must dive into the particulars of the situation to understand the nature of the privilege and other expressions of Hohfeldian concepts that exist even for the same agent.

2.2.3   Power and Liability

This second set of Hohfeldian relations is known as secondary relations. These essentially serve as potential modifiers of the primary legal positions. These secondary jural or legal relations are often crucial in understanding how an agent can alter a situation in their favor (Barker, 2018). The ability to exert power can be a crucial form of economic value or influence and leverage.

A Hohfeldian **power** is the ability of an agent to change their legal standing vis-à-vis another agent. The holder of a Hohfeldian power may or may not exercise that power. The exercise of power likely depends on a number of external conditions as well as the internal preferences and feelings of the agent. The impact of the exercise of power by agent Alpha on agent Beta can result in two scenarios: (1) agent Beta moves from a liability to a duty to act or not act in a certain fashion or (2) agent Beta moves from a liability to their own power status as to whether to act or not.

In scenario 1, agent Alpha may have the power to engage in a transaction with agent Beta (who in turn has a liability). For example, agent Alpha may have the power to offer a contract to agent Beta for certain goods or services. Now, the legal relations have changed between the agents. In this case, agent beta now has the power to act and change the legal relations again and certify or agree to the contract or turn it down, which in either case results in a change in legal relations. Scenario 2 would occur when agent Alpha may have the power in some situations to turn a correlated liability into a duty on agent Beta.

A **liability** is the other side of the relationship from a power. If agent Alpha has a Hohfeldian power, this means that an agent Beta can have their legal relationship altered by agent Alpha. This does not mean that an agent Beta who has a liability will be economically harmed per se by having to enter into this transaction or relationship. The word "liability" should not be interpreted in this context as is more typically the case such as a debt owed. In other words, an agent in a position of Hohfeldian liability does not necessarily or automatically mean that this agent will be financially worse off if a power is exercised.

Once the power is exercised and the legal relationship is altered between agents, a new analysis of the situation must be undertaken. The exercise of power also extinguishes the liability side of the reciprocal relationship for agent Beta. It is crucial for the analyst to consider each individual situation separately and in the context of the decisions made.

A liability refers to the potential lack of control in a given situation at being subject to the power of another economic agent. For example, in Example 2.2, we might also consider how your legal relationship changes before the lease for the apartment is signed. Prior to receiving the document, you have no legal relationship with the landlord. Yet with the landlord's tendering of the contract, you now have the power to change your legal relationship, and the landlord has liability to you potentially making the change. No legal relation is without its correlative, or the other end of the stick.

2.2.4   Disability and Immunity

The final secondary legal position correlates are immunity and disability. These correlatives are directly related to the power-liability relationship. Similar to a right-duty and privilege-exposure relationship, an economic agent can move from one position to another within this matrix.

A **disability** is a legal relation whereby agent Alpha moves from a situation of having power relative to agent Beta to having that same power ended. At this point, agent Alpha would not be able to change their legal relationship relative to agent Beta.

For example, in a public accommodation business, agent Alpha does, under many circumstances, have the power to impose on agent Beta and demand access to the good or service. However, if agent Alpha does not have the money to pay for the good or service, they would then potentially be at a disability to change the legal relationship and have access to the good or service. A disability means that an agent Alpha is prohibited by the going concern from preventing or interfering with the actions of another agent Beta in the concern.

An **immunity** is the legal relation where the power agent Alpha has relative to agent Beta ends and agent Beta is not exposed to a potential change in their legal relationship vis-à-vis agent Alpha. At some point, due to any number of factors, agent Alpha may shift from a liability to an immunity. An immunity, the correlative of disability, means that agent Beta is protected from the actions in that specific arena. If agent Alpha has an immunity, they cannot be legally damaged by another agent(s) Beta who is disabled in this regard. It should also be clear that agent Beta being immune from action by Alpha is again one sided; it implies nothing about what actions agent Beta may or may not do. Again, the emphasis is on the joint determination of the relationship of the parties to one another.

In using this conceptual framework, one must keep in mind the various relationships of the concepts to each other and how they apply to the agents in the situation. By carefully specifying the key relationships amongst agents in a situation, the analyst can begin to understand the incentives towards action that exist and may or may not be exercised.

Example 2.3
A Utah statute limited mining labor to eight hours a day per worker. Anderson, a worker at a Utah mine, was fired by the mine owner after he refused to work over the eight-hour limit. Anderson lodged a complaint and the local sheriff Hardy arrested the mine owner (Holden). Imagine that the issue was taken

Table 2.2   Anderson v. Holden (in favor of Anderson)

Anderson	Holden
Right to not work more than H > 8	Duty to not fire for H = 8
Privilege to leave at H = 8	Exposure to not stop (fire) for H < 8
Power to have Holden arrested by Hardy	Liability in the form of potential arrest or fine
Immunity from firing	Disability (no power) to fire

to court by Holden, who contested the arrest. Who has rights here? Who has power?

There are several background elements to this case. The most obvious is whether or not the plaintiff (Holden) actually fired Anderson for refusing to work more than the legally limited eight hours per day, or if he can argue that he was fired for other reasons. The other issue is whether or not Anderson could have Holden arrested. Let us assume it is already proven (or reasonably assumed) that Holden fired Anderson specifically over hours worked. Consider what each decision might say about the present bundle of rights. Consider how the Hohfeldian matrix would play out were the judge to find in favor of Anderson and Hardy in Table 2.2.

We see that Anderson's right to his eight-hour or less workday has more to do with Holden's corresponding duty not to fire him if he does not work more. Anderson has the privilege to leave after his eight hours are completed, and Holden cannot stop him. Each of these individuals has limits on their jural relations. Anderson's right to an eight-hour or less workday ends when he is exposed to Holden's privilege to fire him if he works less. Holden's duty to not fire Anderson similarly ends when his privilege to fire for other reasons, or for working less, begins.

The second part of this analysis is whether Anderson has the power to have Holden arrested by the officer Hardy. While it is possible for the rule to be on the books that supports the eight-hour or less workday *without* the court ruling that Anderson had the power to have Holden arrested, this too has implications for the initial right/duty matrix discussed above. Consider how this matrix might change if the judge found for Holden instead (Table 2.3).

Decisions regarding power can have many implications in our courts. Whether an agent (or plaintiff) is determined to have legal standing to bring suit in court is directly related to whether they have power or not (see Appendix G for more on understanding legal briefs and the American legal system). If it were found that Anderson did not have the legal standing to have Holden arrested by Hardy, for instance, his "right" to leave after working his eight hours would be an empty one, until such a time as other avenues of enforcement became clear (which may not happen). If Anderson has no power

Table 2.3   Anderson v. Holden (in favor of Holden)

Anderson	Holden
Duty to work H > 8 or risk being fired	Right to enforce H > 8
Exposure to firing if working H < 8	Privilege to fire
Liability (lost income, job)	Power to withhold work/wages
Disability (no power) to regain job	Immunity to arrest/fine

and Holden is immune to arrest for this offense, Anderson is in a significantly disadvantaged situation.

Issues of legal standing and who has the ability to enforce and to bring suit make up a large portion of jural decisions today. It is common for a case to turn on whether an agent has standing rather than the details of the initial complaint or alleged transgression. In a 2021 Supreme Court decision (*TransUnion* v. *Ramirez*) regarding credit agencies, for instance, the supreme court put new limits on who was eligible to sue when inaccurately labeled a terrorist on their credit reports (Howe, 2021a). The issue revolved around when and how a plaintiff had to show injury to have legal standing to sue a defendant. Cases such as these present an entirely different angle from which to consider jural relations.

2.3   APPLYING HOHFELD: A FAMILIAR CASE

Recall the example of the doctor and the candy maker given by Coase (1960) in his famous article "The problem of social cost." He described the case (*Sturges* v. *Brickman*) of two agents operating separate businesses in offices side by side (Figure 2.2): a doctor, looking for a stable, quiet environment in which to treat patients, and a candy maker, utilizing the space for his or her craft, accompanied by the noisy machinery (as was the technology of that time) necessary to do so. The doctor and candy maker had property next door to each other for many years. The piece of property the doctor owned next to the candy maker's shop was originally a garden but then was converted into a visiting room for the doctor's patients. The candy maker used a series of mortars to make the goods he produced and these made a significant amount of noise and vibration. This noise made it nearly impossible for the doctor to operate his visiting room.

Coase uses the case to demonstrate externalities in his larger discussion of transaction costs, or the cost of any kind of bargaining or solution finding on the part of the doctor. The focus of commentary on the paper has been on the external effect of the machines, or the noise created. The subsequent questions center around who should bear the cost of any noise-remediating activity, or

Business Park

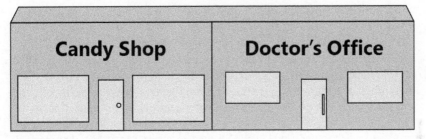

Figure 2.2   Doctor v. candy maker

the cost of exiting the situation all together (should doctor or candy maker be forced or compensated in some way to pack up and move elsewhere). But the focus on the noise, or the "external" effect of the machines in this case, is not whole. It is true that when a candy maker goes about his work with the help of his noisy machines, he causes a problem for the doctor next door. If the machines were not there, the doctor would have peace. Yet if the doctor was not there, the machines would not be a problem. Ceasing the "harm" the candy maker is doing to the doctor would harm the candy maker. Allowing it to continue harms the doctor. The root of the issue is that the doctor and the candy maker are interdependent, each wishing to utilize that same "noise space" differently, not that there is an "external" effect of the machines. This fundamental interdependence or reciprocity is a common theme for both Coase and Hohfeld.

In a Hohfeldian sense, each agent can be thought of as having a bundle of rights (duties) and privileges (exposures) to use their space. One of those sticks in the bundle is a right to other agents not trespassing in the space they are occupying. The agents also have a privilege to operate a business or other occupation assuming they meet relevant business licensing or other require-ments. A privilege in this case means they can operate their respective busi-nesses and that others may be exposed to damages without remedy (exposure). That said, the analyst needs to consider the jural relations from both parties' perspectives. The doctor has a privilege to operate and the candy maker has a privilege to operate, but in this case the two privileges (and exposures) clash with one another.

The status quo situation was that the candy maker had the privilege to continue to operate and the doctor was held to be exposed to that privilege. However, prior to the doctor's actions, there was no conflict. The doctor then used their privilege to alter their property. However, upon the exercise of this privilege, the doctor and candy maker came into conflict. In this new situation, the doctor was facing a loss of income and opportunity relative to the candy maker as the noise prevented the doctor from operating.

At the same time, the status quo situation, as is often the case, created a tension that could potentially lead to change. We can imagine the two of them arguing about who had what right to operate and under what conditions. The doctor in this case sued the candy maker claiming that he in fact had a Hohfeldian right to operate and that the candy maker was in fact under a Hohfeldian duty to not interfere with the doctor's operations. Initially, the English courts ruled in favor of the doctor and placed an injunction on the candy maker's operations. On appeal, the English courts upheld the injunction as valid and the candy maker was forced to cease operations. The doctor's Hohfeldian right had been affirmed by the judicial system and the candy maker had a duty to cease operating.

Regardless of the actual outcome of the case, the point of reciprocity is crucial. This is just the beginning of how Hohfeldian legal analysis could be applied. When we adopt this concept of the dual nature of institutions, we gain greater specificity and clarity of the structural component of institutional analysis. Importantly, there is no clear answer in this case with a reference to economic efficiency or similar performance criteria. The real question is who gets to impose costs on whom.

It should be clear by now that these jural correlatives are an important analytical tool for working in the institutional economics mindset. They also provide a sharp distinction to the standard economic approach to constraints and opportunity sets. We are often instructed that a constraint or limitation exists on one party, be it a consumer or producer, which shapes their utility-maximizing or profit-maximizing decisions. These constraints are typically revealed to come from a consumer's overall budget or a firm's production/cost function. Through the use of the Hohfeldian approach, we can observe that in fact part of the consumer's budget constraint or firm's production/cost function comes from its legal relations with other parties. In other words, one party's constraint or disablement refers directly to one or more other parties' correlating set of legal relations. The analyst must consider both sides of the transaction and not just whether a constraint exists on one party to fully appreciate how changes in policy relate to changes in opportunity or income for all stakeholders.

2.4   SOME ADDITIONAL CONSIDERATIONS IN HOHFELD'S SYSTEM

The Hohfeld system is based on defining specific legal relations as understood at a given point in time. Of course, parties may dispute their perception of the legal relations and this may lead to discussion and even the activation of the legal arbitration process. The discussion and debate over legal relations may be subject to each party's calculator as to how far to push a dispute. Each level of dispute or conflict resolution process incurs costs and carries very real implications for economic performance. At whatever level of dispute the parties pursue, this is where the final disposition of legal relations will land. A decision in court may resolve the set of jural correlatives and set some degree of precedence as to how future parties should understand their legal standing in relation to one another.

Through all of this, the parties' psychology or orientation towards the issue plays a key role. If one party is acting in an altruistic manner, this will have important implications for the final resolution of the transaction or dispute. We talk more about conduct (or behavioral assumptions) in Chapter 4 as we build our framework for institutional impact analysis.

The Hohfeldian matrix of legal relations enables us to analyze the institutions at play in any given situation. It offers an alternate, non-discrete method for defining "rights" that enables the analyst to conduct institutional analysis centered on the key issue of interdependence. In Chapter 3, we use these building blocks to show how more complex legal relations are formed, and how they interact with each other, looking back and connecting to more familiar legal terminology. Going forward, it is important to remember that these bundles of rights and other legal relations are used to represent the institutions themselves, forming the structural piece of any institutional impact analysis. This structural piece of institutional analysis then allows us to imagine a change in those institutions and the subsequent performance characteristics of each institutional alternative. This forms the backbone of the LEP framework as introduced in Chapter 4. In Part II of this text, we apply this Hohfeldian model for thinking about institutional structure to a series of unique situations of interdependence.

THINK ABOUT IT ...
The Bill of Rights as Negative Rights

Think about the first amendment:

> Congress shall make no law respecting an establishment of religion, or prohibiting the free exercise thereof; or abridging the freedom of speech, or of the press; or the right of the people peaceably to assemble, and to petition the Government for a redress of grievances. (Constitution of U.S., 1789 (rev. 1992))

The amendment itself is an example of a **negative right**. Negative right, or negative freedom, means freedom from something. Your negative right imposes a negative duty on others, meaning a duty to do nothing and not interfere. My negative freedom requires only that you respect the right by not preventing me from doing it. Examples of negative rights are the right to live, freedom of speech, freedom of religion, freedom from violence, freedom from slavery and property rights. This negative right represents a specific form of a Hohfeldian duty with reference to the duty being placed typically on government in the case of the U.S. to refrain from interfering in citizens' rights. This is in contrast to a positive freedom or right where the duty holder must do something in the affirmative. For example, some states have a right to education meaning that those state governments are under a positive right of some kind to ensure that students receive some form of education.

Even negative rights have limits, however. For instance, in *Roberts vs. United States Jaycees*, the court found that a regulation furthering state interests (in this case, the enforcement of Minnesota's anti-discrimination Act) could be a valid restriction on freedom of association if it does not suppress significantly more freedom than is necessary to achieve the goal.

Connect ideas
In the case of the first amendment, this negative right also functions as a rule for making rules. Any subsequent laws or rules passed or made by government entities must not infringe on the rights listed in the amendment. Notably, the amendment itself does not say anything about protecting your rights to religion, speech, etc. from your fellow citizens. It simply states what the congress of the U.S. must not do, including passing any law that would keep you from petitioning the government should you feel they failed.

2.5   CHAPTER RECAP

- Economic activity is guided and shaped by many factors including consumer preferences, budget constraints, technology and legal foundations in the form of institutions. All economic transactions are occurring with a background of legal relations existing between buyers and sellers or other parties in the economy. It is partly this legal framework that informs the nature of interdependence between transacting parties.
- Wesley Hohfeld's framework of jural relations provides a language for understanding the institutional structure of the economy. It also emphasizes the basic nature of our interdependence with one another.
- The basic Hohfeldian framework consists of four pairs of jural correlatives: right/duty, privilege/exposure, power/liability and immunity/disability.

The first two sets are primary relations. The second two sets are known as secondary relations as they exist to modify the primary relations.

- A Hohfeldian **right** is a claim that Beta must do or not do something in relation to Alpha. A **duty** is an obligation that Beta must do or not do something in relation to Alpha.
- A Hohfeldian **privilege** is the ability of Alpha to act in a certain manner without being held liable for damages to others (Beta(s)). Hohfeldian **exposure** is the potential damage without remedy that agent Beta is subject to relative to agent Alpha exercising their privilege.
- A Hohfeldian **power** is the ability of agent Alpha to change their legal standing vis-à-vis another agent. A Hohfeldian **liability** means that an agent Beta can have their legal relationship altered by agent Alpha.
- Under a Hohfeldian **immunity**, Beta's relations to Alpha cannot be legally altered by Alpha. Under a Hohfeldian **disability**, Alpha is unable to change their legal relationship with Beta.
- Each jural position can also be viewed as having its unique opposite. Jural opposites cannot exist for the same person or party for the same act at the same time.
- The Hohfeldian framework is used throughout institutional analysis to describe the institutional structure at work in any given situation.

NOTES

1. As Coase (1992, p. 717) puts it, "what are traded on the market are not, as is often supposed by economists, physical entities, but the rights to perform certain actions, and the rights which individuals possess are established by the legal system."
2. It is well established that Ronald Coase did not actually create the Coase Theorem. That honor goes to George Stigler. Coase had an ambiguous relationship with the theorem that carried his name (Medema, 2020).
3. Wesley Hohfeld was a professor of law at Stanford University from 1905 to 1914 and then Yale University from 1914 to 1918. He died young at age 39. He wrote an influential set of law essays that were published in 1919 as *Fundamental legal conceptions as applied in judicial reasoning and other legal essays* (1920).
4. See Commons (1924).

3.   Applying Hohfeld to economics

Hohfeldian legal analysis provides a different, clearer way of structuring and talking about interdependence. Jural relations provide the fundamental building blocks of a legal-economic approach. Using these building blocks, the student and analyst construct a scaffolding of the legal situation, institutional structure and the potential alternatives available. We can then move beyond these simple legal relations and discover and discuss more complex relationships that may exist for each agent.[1]

This chapter will highlight advanced topics in applying the Hohfeldian legal model to economic analysis as explored by these scholars. We begin with a discussion of the concept of property and the bundle of rights approach to legal relations (that happens to coincide with the Hohfeldian framework of Chapter 2). From this topic, we introduce more complicated compound relations not yet discussed. Section 3.3 has to do with coercion and different ways of thinking about power. We discuss these complicated concepts in brief, ending with a discussion of the second level of Hohfeldian analysis: legal remedies. Once this chapter is completed, students and analysts will be able to apply the Hohfeldian framework more fully in a variety of economic situations.

Refer to Appendix G for definitions of unfamiliar legal terms as you move through this and subsequent chapters.

3.1   LAW AND THE BUNDLE OF RIGHTS

The large role that clearly defined and secure property rights play in encouraging wealth creation and economic development is well accepted in the field of economics. The idea of ownership is often left undefined, however, although generally refers to exclusive use and control of a resource or some other good. From the economist's perspective, exclusive use of a resource allows for the proper alignment of incentives. If an economic agent owns a resource, they are both accountable for costs and the beneficiary of any rewards from the use of that resource. A resource that is not owned or has no exclusive use properties is often considered vulnerable to destructive use.

In the case of problems of resource degradation, analysts' understanding of property rights and their creation and enforcement influences the prescriptions recommended to address them (Schlager and Ostrom, 1992). For example, situations of resource degradation in the face of what is labeled non-ownership (or the incredibly broad concept of lack of exclusive ownership) has been associated with Garret Hardin's "tragedy of the commons." The tragedy of the commons takes place in a situation without rules governing access and use of a resource, where individuals may act independently in accordance with their own best interest even to the detriment of society and ultimate depletion of the resource (Hardin, 1968). Oft-used examples of "commons" from an economic standpoint include any open-access or "unregulated" resource such as grazing lands, fisheries, forests, the atmosphere and even the shared kitchenette or fridge in your workspace. But these examples of commons historically feature aspects of ownership – just not in the exclusive sense often alluded to. This is where thinking about ownership in terms of legal relations – or a bundle of rights – becomes useful.

As described by Schlager and Ostrom (1992), common property in particular is one example of a term prone to describing multiple different analytical situations, including (1) property owned by government, (2) property owned by no one, (3) property owned and defended by a community of resource users and (4) any common-pool resource used by multiple individuals regardless of the type of property rights involved. From a legal standpoint, **common property** is a type of property jointly held and managed through various formal or informal means by members of a community or going concern(s). The term "common property" as employed here refers to a distribution of property rights in resources in which several owners are co-equal in their rights to use the resource, their rights are not lost through non-use, while co-equal owners are not necessarily equal with respect to the quantity (or other aspect) of use over time (Ciriacy-Wantrup and Bishop, 1975). This use right can be extremely specific. It is not an all-consuming right to all aspects of the good, such as the right to transfer, that we traditionally associate with ownership. But it is a form of ownership nonetheless. Similarly, something referred to as the "anti-commons" is a situation where many individuals have exclusion rights to an asset. Each has some degree of ownership over the good and can veto the decisions of others, resulting in issues such as underuse (Boettke and Subric, 2008). This distinction between economic ideas of property (or ownership) and what it means to possess rights to something is key to properly building the Hohfeldian model.[2]

In the legal field, William Blackstone is best known for his association of real property with the idea of ownership.[3] Blackstone, it has been argued, was one of the originators of the idea that an owner of a piece of property had absolute dominion over that object. Robert Burns wrote that Blackstone believed that "property was an absolute right vested in the individual by the immutable law of nature" (Burns, 1985, p. 67). Like the economists of the twentieth century, Blackstone believed that exclusive and absolute control over the piece of property or the object was essential to the idea of property law. Blackstone also wrote that property was the "sole and despotic dominion which one man claims and exercises over the external things in the world in total exclusion of the right of any other individual in the universe" (Di Robliant, 2013, p. 877).

That view of property and property law began to change over time. In 1922, law professor Arthur Crobin wrote (as cited by Di Robliant, 2013) that, "our concept of property has shifted ... property has ceased to describe any real object of sense at all and has become merely a bundle of legal relations – rights, powers, privileges and immunities" (Di Robliant, 2013, p. 877). This means that, from an economic standpoint, ownership may mean many things. Specifying a variable in a binary fashion as owned or not does not capture the full complexity of what the agent can and cannot do with a property.

As explained in Chapter 2, rights are a key legal concept. We learned that when thinking about a rights holder, the analyst needs to look at the other side of the right to the duty holder. The duty holder may be everyone else or one specific person but in either case they are required to do or not do something relative to the rights holder. However, in reality there are many different legal relations at play between two agents for any particular situation. These relations within the situation come in a package, often referred to as a bundle of rights.

From an analytical perspective, the rights bundle needs to be broken down and understood piece by piece. An even more critical point that we have emphasized is the interdependent nature of the economy and law. The bundle of rights metaphor or concept clearly captures that ownership is about relations between people and not about relations between people and objects. The bundle of rights metaphor has been a dominant part of thinking in law and legal training for much of the twentieth century. In the last few decades, this metaphor has increasingly come under attack for a variety of reasons.[4] However, in general terms, the metaphor or concept retains much of this analytical capacity and power.

The bundle of rights approach is most applicable to property law. Property law is defined as the law regarding the ownership of tangible and intangible objects (Legal Information Institute, 2021). As such, it has a massive impact on the economy as a whole. The most common aspects of ownership of property or the bundle of rights as defined by Honore (1961) include:

1. the right of possession and to remain in possession;
2. right to use;
3. right to manage;
4. right to income;
5. right to the capital;
6. right to the security;
7. incident to transmissibility;

8. incident of absence of term;
9. prohibition of harmful use;
10. residuary character; and
11. liability of execution.

Each of these aspects may or may not be present in any specific situation.

The first six characteristics described by Honore rely on a language of rights. Leaning on Hohfeld, we can assume that a reciprocal duty must exist for one or more economic agents for each of these. For example, having a right to manage or earn income from the property serves as an asset or expansion of the opportunity set of that economic agent.

In the next two characteristics, Honore uses the term "incident." This implies that the ownership of an object may have a durational clause related to it. In some cases, an owner may be able to transmit the property or object to all future heirs and in other cases ownership may end with death. The second part of this incidence issue is whether a specific ownership claim continues after a period of time irrespective of death or sale. Although Honore does not use the term "right" in this context, in a general sense the idea of a Hohfeldian right can be used in the case of the bundle of duration.

There are two other interesting aspects of Honore's characteristics of ownership. The first is that owners may actually be under a Hohfeldian duty to not undertake certain activities or uses of their property. The owner may have a right to exclusive use of the property or preventing others from trespass on that property, but that does not in turn lead to unlimited use as a natural corollary. For example, a property owner does not generally own the rights to airspace above the property. The second interesting point is that jural relations will shift if an owner uses the property or object as collateral for a loan or debt agreement. In this case another agent may gain a Hohfeldian power that can be exercised under certain circumstances to retain ownership.

The final couple of characteristics actually include the imposition of a duty on a property owner. The real question of course is who gets to define "harm" in this case. The harm may be defined by any number of conflicting views from a government entity, a court, neighbors and other property owners, etc.

The main takeaway from this discussion is that ownership of a resource is made up of multiple pieces or portions that can be separated from one another. It is necessary to break down and consider what property rights or ownership may mean in any given situation. From an institutional impact analysis standpoint, different regimes will mean that the bundle will be broken down differently for various economic agents. These relations are highly specific to their situation and likely to change over time. For instance, in the case of airspace, it took time as airplanes became widespread to address the issue of who owns the space above a property. The airspace stick in the bundle had to be disaggregated from the overall bundle of traditional property claims. The distribution of the bundle will have important implications for economic performance outcomes.[5]

3.2   COMPOUND LEGAL RELATIONS

Hohfeldian legal and jural relations generally work together and not in isolation of one another. An economic agent typically has multiple or compound rights and duties simultaneously. The analyst will need to carefully consider how each agent is situated within a particular context. For the Hohfeldian framework to be used successfully in analysis, it requires a careful breaking down of each legal or institutional relationship between economic agents in specific cases of interdependence. In the following sections we consider examples of compound legal relations that can coexist at the same time.

3.2.1   Common Right

A Hohfeldian right has been referred to by some authors as a "strict right" in the sense that a "strict" rights holder is in the position that some other party may not do something to them (Sichelman, 2018). In contrast, a common right (also known as a protected privilege), is a privilege combined with a right in the same economic agent. In this case, agent Alpha holds a privilege to do an action and at the same time holds rights against others, such as rights against trespass, assault and nuisance, to prevent interference when exercising that privilege. This contrasts with a situation where an economic agent holds a privilege to do or not take an action but is not protected from the actions of others.

An economic agent Alpha may have the privilege to open and operate a new retail store and another nearby agent Beta may have certain duties of non-interference, albeit with some limits. Beta cannot, for example, use physical force or violence to stop agent Alpha from operating their business. Beta would be allowed to compete in certain ways such as price competition or marketing efforts within limits. There may be a rule placing a duty on Beta (and a right to Alpha) that restricts Beta from lying about Alpha's products or services in advertising. The presence of these conditioning rights/duties (or "background rights") in practice can limit or strengthen the opportunities available to agents.

It may be that every specific point of duty or privilege is not relevant to the analysis. But in many cases, the common right is quite likely present and should be assessed by the analyst. The existence and functioning of a common right, as with the primary and secondary legal relations of the Hohfeldian framework, have important economic performance implications.

3.2.2   Claim

When Hohfeld was writing in the early twentieth century, he discussed a Hohfeldian "claim right." Hohfeld's use of the term in this manner has fallen out of favor. Today, we speak of a "claim" as a compound of several key legal principles (Sichelman, 2018). A modern claim is the combination of two Hohfeldian positions. The two Hohfeldian relations in play for agent Alpha are the breached duty (relative to agent Beta) and the power (contingent) to bring an action to redress the breach. This was something foreseen by economist John R. Commons in his adaptation of Hohfeld (see Commons, 1924; Fiorito, 2010).

The Commons framework included the officials who must act on behalf of or against agent Alpha and Beta to ensure a remedy is carried out for damages done in the case of a violated duty. This closer consideration of remedy is important because it determines whether there is truly a Hohfeldian right present or instead an empty right. An **empty right** occurs when a rights holder does not have any form of remedy. The duty does exist from agent Beta to do or not do an action, but agent Alpha has no recourse. This is very different from a situation in which agent Alpha has undertaken a cost-benefit analysis as to whether or not to use a remedy that is available to them. In the case of an empty right, there is literally no remedy available. For instance, consider a situation in which you are struck by a car. Generally speaking, a person would have a right in this type of situation and can pursue recourse for damages. However, if the car was driven by the president of the U.S., his or her position of immunity from suit or charges might put you in a position of holding an empty right.

This is different from a situation where there is a disability-immunity secondary legal relation. A disability simply means that I cannot change my legal relationship with another economic agent(s). In the example above, I generally have some level of rights if hit by another vehicle and would not be in a position of disability. That said, the two are quite similar or parallel in how we might think of them. The advantage of striving for clarity in documenting the initial legal or institutional relationship that exists is due to the potential for changes in that legal relationship from the agents themselves or from an adjudicatory body such as a court.

3.2.3   Liberty

Another compound concept is known as a **liberty** (Sichelman, 2018). Although some have tried to equate liberty and privilege in the Hohfeldian scheme, this has been argued more recently to be mistaken by other scholars (Sichelman, 2018). The idea is that liberty should only apply to a situation where the agent has both a privilege to do and not do an action (also known as an option in economics and finance). Otherwise, a one-sided privilege to do something or not do something should be contained in the word privilege only. A liberty is thus a dual-sided privilege while a "strict" privilege relates to a one-sided ability to undertake or not undertake an action.

In economics, we have tended to consider only the side of the agent being able to make a choice and the breadth of their choices in a positive sense. However, the "choice" to not do something can be of equal import and of economic value to an agent. We discuss the idea of an opportunity cost of taking one of several possible actions. Less often discussed is the issue of potential value of being able to not take an action.

3.2.4   Compound Rules and Legal Interdependence: Liability, Property, and Inalienability Rules

Another source of advanced topics relates to an expanded sense of what a legal right or duty is and how they interact with each other in compound situations. In 1972, one of the most highly cited articles in all of law and economics was published by Guido Calabresi and A. Douglas Melamed. Their focus was on combining tort law and property law into a common framework and creating a set of rules by which scholars and analysts could understand these systems. The ideas developed by these scholars can help further illuminate the Hohfeldian system and its use in institutional economics. They can help the analyst understand the various institutional structures that may guide the interdependence between economic agents.

Calabresi and Melamed (1972) identified three basic legal rules: (1) property rules, (2) liability rules and (3) inalienability rules. These rules are essentially built from the foundations of a Hohfeldian framework. Their widespread use in the literature makes it important to understand them from this perspective.

Under a property rule, if agent Alpha holds ownership of something then agent Beta or others cannot access or use that property without the consent of agent Alpha. In other words, agent Alpha holds a right against any others who are under a duty not to interfere with or attempt to use the property in question. The property rule is the stronger set of protections to a property or entitlement owner. In the case of the property rule, the owner has in-kind enjoyment of the property, right to monetary compensation from transfers and the initiation choice and veto power (further discussed in Section 3.2.2). The non-owning agents under a property rule regime have no Hohfeldian power to change the legal relationship. The non-owning agent has the privilege to offer to transact with the owning agent. The owning agent can respond or not and is under no obligation or duty to respond.

The general liability rule, in contrast, is one where agent Beta has a privilege and is not under a duty (and agent Alpha does not have a right) to prevent agent Beta from using a particular property object. Agent Alpha, in turn has a privilege of using the property object but does have the legal right to prevent another from using it. Under the liability rule, agent Beta will potentially be under a duty to compensate agent Alpha for use of the property. In this situation, assuming agent Beta has used their privilege to act, Agent Alpha has a Hohfeldian power to potentially act and use an adjudication system to force payment for the use of the property object. Morris (1992) writes that liability rules actually allow one economic agent to use another economic agent's possessions or property at a price that will be determined in some type of conflict resolution process. The initial owning economic agent has the right to enjoy the property and to be properly compensated for use of the property and can initiate a decision to transfer the property.

The liability rule does provide the owner with initiation choice power and the right to in-kind enjoyment of the property and even the right to monetary compensation for a transfer but does not provide the veto power to the property owner. This is an important distinction that must be made. In essence, a liability rule does not protect the property owner fully. Another economic agent may in essence use the property and pay the penalty.

Finally, the inalienability rule means that neither agent Alpha nor Beta can transfer the property to another agent. For example, in the U.S., an economic agent cannot transfer the right of their own body (slavery) to another. In this case, the governing authority, which could be the government or another entity, has decided that certain entitlement or object transfers cannot occur. An inalienability rule means that the veto power and initiation choice are both non-existent for agents. These are entitlements where the rules are such that the owning economic agent has no legal right or power to transfer the entitlement and simultaneously other economic agents have no right or power to force a transfer. In other words, this is a blocked exchange. For some from a libertarian viewpoint, it is an anathema for a blocked exchange to exist except under extreme circumstances. Other viewpoints justify a much wider range of blocked exchanges. Empirically, some societies have increased the number of blocked exchanges as compared to historical circumstances.

In a framework of economic agents and the value of assets or contingent liabilities that they may be holding, understanding these rules and whether they are present will make an important difference in any analysis. A property rule that favors one economic agent will clearly increase the value of the specific assets that they hold and potentially increase the liabilities of the opposite economic agents. A liability rule is of less value and this will likely be reflected in the marketplace for that specific entitlement as there is not pure exclusion. In other words, the liability rule implies that the breaching agent can act and just has to pay a penalty afterwards versus being under a duty, as with a property rule, to not act in the first place.

The critical point to recall is that we again can group and regroup the basic rights and duties of the Hohfeldian framework to understand complex legal relationships in the real world and how these relationships are coded. The basic Hohfeldian framework provides the building blocks for comprehending the complex legal relations that are expressed in real-world transactional relationships. These legal relations are the basis or the starting point for transactions as they occur.

THINK ABOUT IT ...
Accounting Terminology and a Link to Compound Legal Relations

The legal relations as established between agents have an important and direct influence on the distribution of wealth and income and can be expressed in accounting terms. Both income flows and asset stocks can be considered in light of legal relations. Assets for a going concern could include freedom from government restrictions, access to credit, ownership of property or other such items. A Hohfeldian right or privilege (or the compound ideas) can in some cases be expressed as items on the asset side of the balance sheet or the income flow of a going concern.

A Hohfeldian right means that a duty holder must do something, such as make a payment, or refrain from doing something. The holder of a right likely translates into some kind of financial advantage whether it be direct financial benefit or more indirectly, like in a situation where a competitor is prevented from doing something that would harm the right-holding business. A right to keep another from acting would at least increase the value of a business or a household balance sheet even if it does not result in a direct financial payment.

The economic value of a Hohfeldian privilege depends on the type of privilege being held by the agent. A strict privilege may not garner a great degree of value but a protected privilege that includes the right of non-interference could be more valuable. That should be reflected in the value or price of the asset as demonstrated on the balance sheet (all other factors being equal).

A Hohfeldian duty is clearly not financially beneficial to an economic agent. The number of duties imposed and the greater degree of coercion mean that those producers' or households' overall economic value and income flow is likely greatly reduced relative to other agents.

A Hohfeldian liability to a legal relations change is more complicated but can be viewed in a relative light. If the agent with a liability holds a veto power, the liability itself would not necessarily be that harmful as the process can be halted. The lack of a veto power could be more problematic and lead to a downgrading of the overall economic value of that agent in a relative sense.

There is not always direct correlation between Hohfeldian jural positions and income and wealth variables. An analyst must be careful to consider all the potential ramifications of the various legal positions in any given situation. Sometimes, a Hohfeldian position may be clearly beneficial relative to other agents such as in the case of a right or duty. In other cases, the existence of power, liability and immunity relations may be less clear. The analyst needs to consider the relationship between wealth and income distribution and how alternative institutional regimes drive these factors.

3.3 POWER, COERCION AND HOHFELDIAN POWER

Economic agents do not have equal power in their interactions and interdependence. Power differentials are often described as to blame for many of the major differences we see in income, health and wealth distribution, among other differences. Issues of power, both political and economic, are among some of the most pressing topics at the center of social discourse both historically and in the present day.

Economists have typically thought about power primarily in the context of market power between producers and consumers. The standard neoclassical economics model discusses market power and the ability of one economic agent to exert influence on prices. The primary focus of the standard model is on the power of producers to influence the market in their own favor and capture consumer surplus. Economists often discuss the need for robust competition to address market power concerns and in some cases government action via anti-trust law. However, this is not the only way to think about economic power.

3.3.1 Further Thoughts on Hohfeldian Power

As an analyst uses the Hohfeldian model, they must be aware that exercise of power and the resulting coercion in transactions and interactions are not in most cases based on an equal distribution of rights and other Hohfeldian jural positions. These differences can be extremely important in understanding the impact of alternative institutional regimes.

Economic power is defined as the ability of one economic agent to exert direct or indirect influence on the decisions of other economic agents in any context. For example, it has been argued that the ability of one economic agent to impose opportunity costs on another party is an important measure of economic power (Samuels and Schmid, 2005). **Coercion** is the resulting impact on agents from those who use power. In this way of thinking, an economic agent who has little ability to impose costs on others has minimal power and is being coerced by other agents. In any economic situation, there is likely to be a degree of differential power between economic agents.

How does power come into play in the Hohfeldian system? Hohfeld used the term "power" to refer to the ability of an economic agent to change their legal relations relative to one or more other economic agents. Let us unpack this concept. To clarify, a right is distinguished from a power in the fact that the right holder's actions or lack of actions is irrelevant for the analysis – it is the duty side (or what others must or must not do) that matters in a rights context. In a situation of legal power, the issue is that the power holder has the ability to make a decision. They are not mandated to do anything, only that they can do something. There are many examples of an economic agent exercising a legal power. This could include entering a contract, selling title to land, establishing a trust, buying a product from a retailer and many others. The core similarity of these situations is that the economic agent has the power to make a decision and act, and in so doing, change their legal relations with another agent.

The other side of the Hohfeldian power is a liability position. This agent is subject to having their legal relations changed relative to the potential power-exercising agent. Again, a liability should not be interpreted in the financial sense of automatically being a negative position. There are many situations where a change in legal status may mean a financial gain for agent Beta. What is true, however, is that agent Beta cannot act to prevent their legal status from being altered or changed, or at least cannot until agent Alpha has acted first.

We can provide some useful clarification of the concept of Hohfeldian power by distinguishing between voluntary and volitional choice and control (Reilly, 2019). In his writing, Hohfeld used the term volitional control when referring to a legal power. Volition simply refers to the concept of "using one's will" and control means exercising or doing something. Therefore, a Hohfeldian power can be thought of as a situation where an economic agent can make a decision about a course of action that is to some degree intentional. One way to think about this is the difference between voluntary choice and volitional choice. Voluntary choice is a choice situation where only physical or natural constraints exist. Volitional choice is where an economics agent's opportunities are prevented not just by physical constraints but by the choices and decisions of others. As the power of economic agent Alpha to impact economic agent Beta increases, the volitional choices of agent Beta are reduced or eliminated. Thus, in modeling a specific situation, we can examine how the power of one side or the other is used to prevent options for the other agent(s).

3.3.2   Initiation Choice and Veto Power

Some have argued that further information is needed to truly understand the nature of legal power in an economic relationship. The analyst will need to decide when such further information is needed to truly understand a situation. For example, as discussed earlier, the jural correlative to Hohfeldian power is a liability. The agent or agents on the other side of the potential exercise of power are at a Hohfeldian liability to have their legal status changed. Agent Alpha may be able to exercise power, under certain conditions, and change their legal status vis-à-vis agent Beta. If agent Alpha offers a contract to agent Beta, places agent Beta's name into a will or any number of other decisions, agent Beta who was at a liability prior to the exercise of power has now had their legal relationship altered with agent Alpha. The question is what does that mean for agent Beta? A further specification of the Hohfeldian model can help us understand these economic situations and how the exercise of power then plays out between the agents.

Morris (1992) provided another important expansion of the Hohfeldian jural relations related to these diverse types of rules and some further iterations that can be considered in analysis. She writes that power and immunity are related to "the realm of control over transfer of 'entitlements'" (Morris, 1992, p. 833). But who has what form of power in each situation? Morris enlarges our vocabulary with the ideas of "initiation choice" and "veto power."

Initiation choice is the specific power of one or another economic agent to begin the potential transfer process. For example, the initiation of choice power means that the holder of the object or entitlement (agent Alpha) can make an offer to another (agent Beta) for a transfer. During the offer period, agent Beta now has the legal power to transform the legal relationship between the agents by accepting the offer and agent Alpha is now under a liability. There is no requirement that one or both agents hold an ability to initiate a transfer of power.

The initiation choice does not mean that a transfer will occur but rather that a potential transfer is possible. Whether a transfer of an entitlement or object will occur depends at least partially on the existence of veto power for the economic agent on the opposite side of the transaction. Veto power is another form of Hohfeldian power and is the opposite side of initiation choice and dictates who can stop a transfer from happening. One or both agents may have a Hohfeldian veto power. The lack of a veto power means that the particular economic agent would be under a Hohfeldian duty to act if an opposing agent exercised power and changed their legal relationships. Of course, having veto power does not imply whether one will or will not use the ability to veto a transaction.

With initiation choice and veto power, we have the ability to further examine a situation and its legal foundations and how the various opportunity sets and choice constraints exist for each of the interacting economic agents. For example, a buy-sell agreement is fairly typical in limited liability partnerships and other corporate forms in some cases. These agreements specify when the owners or partners can buy or sell to each other and under what conditions. If one owner (agent Beta) falls under certain conditions (say is forced to file bankruptcy), the other owners or partners (agent Alpha) gain a legal power to force a sale to them. If agent Alpha exercises this power, the bankruptcy owner may not have a veto power to stop the transfer. Here, we see that one set of agents can have initiation power while the other agent lacks veto power to stop the transfer. The transfer will still result in some value to the bankruptcy owner but likely under conditions that they cannot negotiate.

3.3.3   From Hohfeldian Power to Disability

It is important to emphasize that the ability to exercise a power by agent Alpha is not unlimited or unconditional and may switch to a disability and immunity set of positions in some cases. Under certain conditions or scenarios, agent Alpha switches from a status of power to a status of disability and agent Beta moves from liability to immunity. The power-holding agent in any given situation is not automatically immune from having that volitional or decisional control taken away from them. There are institutional arrangements or regimes whereby another agent or entity could divest that power from an economic agent. The main takeaway is that the existence of a Hohfeldian power, as with other basic components of the Hohfeldian model, does not imply that other elements automatically exist. The context must be investigated by the analyst. Unlike the standard economic model of budget constrained choice, there are many elements of choice to explore when law is brought from the background to the foreground of economic decision making.

3.3.4   Institutional Alternatives, Impact Analysis and Coercion

In institutional impact analysis, different regimes may in one case expand the Hohfeldian power of agent Alpha relative to agent Beta and vice versa in another regime. Each of these institutional regimes would then have very different economic performance outcomes. In impact analysis with a focus on distributional outcomes between agents, the analyst would need to focus on examining how each institutional or legal alternative shifts the source of power between agents. It would also be useful to assess which type of power is present, starting with perhaps initiation choice and veto power, to determine how various agents would fare under different scenarios.

Power is at least partially a function of the legal and institutional structure of the economy. The institutional system legitimizes certain power-exercising functions over other alternatives. In doing so, the system of **mutual coercion** is established. Mutual coercion is an important term because each side is clearly trying to gain the advantage relative to others in the economy.

Hale (1923) described the economy as a system of "mutual coercion." This implies for example that both sides are able to try and exert their influence in a bargaining situation. Hale defined coercion specifically as the ability of one economic agent to close off or withdraw options from another party. In other words, an economic agent can exert control or coercive force over another economic agent by reducing their opportunity set or imposing opportunity costs on the other party. Hale was also forceful in writing that the power of the government is used to enforce the power of one economic agent relative to another agent. This does not mean that economic actions between agents become a zero-sum game. Both parties may still benefit from the undertaking of an exchange or trade. However, the distribution of benefits and costs in a given situation may be quite skewed and unequal. The analyst should think of coercion not as physical force only, but as the use of power to close off options – or in the language of Hohfeld to reduce privilege or in particular increase duty.

If an analyst wishes to assess the determinants of institutional change (a topic we generally aren't focused on in this book), there are many sources of the unequal distribution of power in legal relations. The accumulation of resources or assets are one source of power differences. This is not the only source of power. Economic agents may inherit power based on their position within an organization. In any case, economic agents will clearly often seek a change in institutions to empower themselves and create liabilities for others as this is a source of wealth and income. There is a large literature on these issues which will not be covered here. However, the Hohfeldian language can enrich our understanding of the type of institutional changes that are being sought.

In Example 3.1, we consider a pivotal court case that involved issues of power and coercion.

Example 3.1

In the famous 1905 legal case, *Lochner* v. *New York* (see Appendix C for case brief), a bakery employer, John Lochner, was fined by an inspector of the state of New York for attempting to require bakery employees to work more than eight hours. In 1895, the state of New York had passed a law that made it illegal (New York Bakeshop Act), with state enforcement, to require bakery employees to work more than ten hours a day and 60 hours a week along with other health and safety provisions. The law stated that a bakery employee in the state of New York was neither "required nor permitted to work in a bakery more than sixty hours" (Urofsky, 2018). Thus, here we see the bakery employees had the legal power to accept an employment contract with an employer but did not have the power to accept a contract or accept conditions after the contract that required working more than 60 hours a week. This situation meant that bakery employees and employers both lacked the initiation choice to override the 60-hour restriction even if they wished to do so. It was a blocked exchange above 60 hours a week.

Mr. Lochner sued the state of New York's labor department for violating his rights to freedom of contract under the fourteenth amendment of the U.S. Constitution. The New York attorney general argued that the state was exercising its police power and its legitimate authority to protect the health and safety of the bakery employees. Here, we observe that the state of New York is the entity acting in remedial fashion to attempt to protect the rights provided to the employees under law. The state of New York exercised its "police" power in a Hohfeldian sense to cause a change in the legal relations with Mr. Lochner by enforcing a coerced punishment with the force of law.

Remember, Hohfeldian power is about the ability of an economic agent to act or make a decision. One could imagine a situation where one economic agent Alpha is using power to restrict the choices of another agent Beta. This could take the form of imposing greater duties or reducing the privilege of agent Beta. Agent Beta's options of movement and conduct are restricted or become more costly as agent Alpha increases their power. In the case of *Lochner* (1905), the bakery employers and employees are both trying to exert their rights and powers to act relative to the other agent.

The U.S. Supreme Court decided in favor of the employers. The majority argument was that the freedom of contract under the fourteenth amendment meant that bakery employees and employers should be able to bargain together and decide hours. These agreements without "state interference" were presumed to be economically efficient as both parties entered into the agreement voluntarily and without coercion (in the physical sense). But is that the only kind of coercion we should worry about? The *Lochner* (1905) decision restructured the economy and, in Hale's words, led to a different form of mutual coercion.

Using institutional impact analysis, as explored fully in Chapter 4, we would start with an understanding of the economic and legal situation and then explore the possible regimes that could structure the interdependence between employers, employees and the state. One regime is, as decided by the U.S. Supreme Court, that the bakery employers gained the Hohfeldian power to offer an employment contract or employment terms with more than 60 hours. At the same time, under freedom of contract terms, the bakery employees were given the Hohfeldian power to accept the terms of employment if they so wished. Of course, the terms of power in this case are not equal. Bakeries are fewer than employees and clearly had the upper hand in negotiations with bakery employees who may not have many other employment options.

In thinking about impact analysis, the first-order analysis would consider how alternatives would create a world where there are more satisfied bakery employees with fewer hours and more restrictions on the volitional choices of employers. There are of course secondary and long-term implications to consider such as the impact of a restriction on working hours of production of bakery goods and the prices of those goods and even the wages paid to employees. There may be some bakery employees who are not happy with these restrictions. All these second-order implications may occur over time and can be considered as well. In any case, each set of institutional and legal regimes, whether it be one in favor of the employers or employees, will result in a different distribution of wealth, income and resources. Each of these distributions is Pareto efficient and Pareto non-comparable.

3.4   LEGAL REMEDIES (ENFORCEMENT)

In situations where a given economic agent believes that their rights have been violated by another party, the method of seeking legal remedy, or enforcement of their right(s), becomes important. This enforcement itself is a series of legal relations. In a contract dispute or in a case of one agent seeking damages or a change in action by another agent, the courts or other adjudication body may need to both decide if a breach of contract or damages has occurred. The **legal remedy** is the ability of one agent to receive compensation or stop the actions of another agent (or both in some cases) if a breach or damages has occurred.

The enforcement of rights or legal remedies constitutes the full scope of how the law and the legal system impact the economy and economic performance. It has long been argued that a violation of legal rights must be accompanied by a legal enforcement mechanism for those rights (Zeigler, 1986). The enforcement of a rights violation can come from private economic agents themselves or from government action in some cases. The U.S. Supreme Court has set complex guidelines and tests for whether a private right of action exists for an agent in the event of a perceived violation (Zeigler, 1986). Enforcement can include criminal and civil penalties and actions, although only the government agent is presumed to have the power to invoke criminal penalties and enforcement which includes physical coercion. In general, economic agents often face a high degree of uncertainty in many cases in determining whether there is any effective remedy in terms of federal legislation and judicial review.

Where the first tier of the Hohfeldian framework determines the primary legal relations that exist between agents in a situation under investigation, a second-tier analysis can be conducted to analyze remedies. In some cases, the agents may utilize a court engagement or mediation to determine where in fact the rights and duties lie in each situation. Once the dispute is resolved in determining where the rights and duties of the parties exist, remedies for a breach can be explored. What happens if an agent is in breach? What are the consequences? If no remedy exists, it may be said that a right has no meaning or is an "empty right."

We focus on the legal-type remedies and enforcement that are available due to a breach of a right. This is quite different from the "remedy" that might be available or used if someone violates a cultural norm or the breach of an informal institution. A remedy analysis is still undertaken using the Hohfeldian jural correlatives and opposites structure. We discuss common legal types below.

If a party feels that a right has been breached, the first part of the second-tier remedial analysis is to identify to whom and under what conditions a remedy is available. In some cases, the potentially aggrieved party may have the power to engage in legal action such as filing a lawsuit to force a remedy. The filing of a lawsuit inevitably involves a complex set of calculations and issues that will challenge the aggrieved agent.

Civil enforcement or remedies can roughly be broken down into two general categories known as (1) liability rules and (2) property rules (Calabresi and Melamed, 1972). As mentioned early in the chapter, a liability rule is one where monetary compensation is ordered by a court to penalize a breaching party (tort damages). The enforcement and remedy in the case of torts and liability are financial payments due to damage caused. A property rule is one where the alleged breaching party is under the potential for some type of direct command to stop or undertake an action. In legal terms, this may be a form of injunction to do or stop doing something. An injunction is a court order that, if violated, can lead to civil and criminal penalties.

The choice of remedies among these options is not a neutral question. A liability rule may benefit certain plaintiffs over others depending on the circumstances. Also, a party may feel that monetary compensation is not enough and that some form of non-monetary compensation (including and up to physical coercion and imprisonment) may be necessary sentences for the wrongs alleged to have been committed.

Another key point of the analysis in considering the remedies for enforcement of breach is the implications or consequences for the various parties involved in the situation of interdependence. Any set of powers and liabilities established in a remedy situation will involve costs and benefits for all of the parties involved and those will be differentiated under different remedy schemes. The analyst should consider the first- and second-tier level of Hohfeldian analysis together (Schlag, 2015).

3.4.1   Private and Public Action of Remedy Enforcement

The question of incentives and actions regarding enforcement must partly come back to who has legal entitlement to undertake action to enforce a law. If an economic agent believes an unlawful act has occurred against them, the next question is who has the Hohfeldian power to bring about an enforcement action to the adjudication system. In some cases, the economic agent may be able to take actions themselves (private right of action) and in other cases, the economic agent may need to use a Hohfeldian power to call on a government agent to take action on their behalf (public right of action).

A private right of action means that a private economic agent, a non-government official, has an implied or express right of action to enforce the breach of law. An implied private right of action means a private economic agent has the privilege to undertake an enforcement action although it is not written in the plain language of a statutory or constitutional document. Implied private rights of actions are created by the courts and not Congress or legislative bodies in general in the U.S. (Bermeo, 2017). An express private right of action means that there is explicit language that a private economic agent has explicit privilege to undertake enforcement action.

The literature has argued that there are several key benefits to having a private right of action (Sant'Ambrogio, 2019). One of those benefits is the reduction of costs to the government for bringing suits against alleged unlawful behavior. A second benefit is that government regulatory bodies may be captured by the very groups that they regulate and are therefore willing to overlook problematic behavior. Another benefit is that the aggrieved agent has more information about the situation and can more efficiently seek enforcement of the action. If no private right of action exists, the government will have to collect and translate information from these private economic agents. Finally, the private right of action provides a venue for smaller or less powerful agents to have their voice heard in court where government action may be lacking.

A public right of action is enforcement by a government official.[6] Of course, the specifics of public action matter as well. Various state and federal laws will have various stipulations as to when a government official can act. These details will play a role in the decision of a government official as to whether to carry out an enforcement action.

Each of these institutional alternatives can have important economic implications. Lack of an express or even implied private right of action means that the alleged victim of an unlawful action may lack a Hohfeldian right to enforcement. This in turn may mean that the primary Hohfeldian right is an empty right. If a private right of action does exist, the aggrieved party is in turn in a stronger bargaining position to demand compensation or another action to address damages.

Public rights of action or government executive/agency enforcement of law is viewed as a better institutional alternative under a different set of arguments. In an idealized world view, the public enforcement of law is better because government officials will take account of social and private cost of an enforcement action whereas a private right of action will only take account of private cost and benefits. Further, an argument against private rights of action is that the allegedly aggrieved agent may take aggressive action to force costs of the other agent(s) in an attempt to force a settlement and thus increase private and social costs.

The trade-offs and incentives regarding the Hohfeldian power of economic agents to a private right of action are also influenced by access to resources and wealth status. Lower-income agents would have much greater difficulty in incurring the opportunity costs of a private right to action. There are both time costs and monetary costs that would have to be considered. Some agents, due to racial or other forms of discrimination in society, may face hurdles and barriers to accessing the adjudication or judicial system to seek redress for economic damages (for an example see Macdowell, 2014). Evidence suggests that low-income agents are often at a major disadvantage to other economic agents in housing, small claims and family courts in the U.S. Low-income advocates have discussed changes in adjudication rules (another form of institution) to address this issue such as paperwork simplification, poor peoples' courts, self-help programs and the use of non-attorney advocates. These changes in the Hohfeldian framework would amount to a change in the secondary jural relation increasing or expanding the power field relative to other more economically powerful economic agents.

For the institutional economics analyst, the key focus is on cultivating an understanding of the trade-offs and arguments concerning private versus public rights of action. These basic enforcement questions play an important role in establishing those secondary Hohfeldian jural relations and the basis for economic decision making. The ability of an agent to undertake a private right of action creates a secondary Hohfeldian power that has potential economic value and the other agent faces a liability. Alternatively, the inability to undertake a private right of action is a Hohfeldian disability for the private agent and an immunity from the point of the other economic agent. This does not preclude a potential public right of action.

3.5   SOURCES OF INTERDEPENDENCE

Another advanced topic in the application of the Hohfeldian model relates to the nature or sources of interdependence that can occur between economic agents. This issue was raised in Chapter 1 and is provided with more context here.

As stated previously, interdependence can come from at least two sources including the legal status quo and physical and biological characteristics of the economic goods under consideration or, as often occurs, some combination of the two. The various sources can guide the analyst as they seek to uncover the legal relations that matter.

Institutional economist Al Schmid focused our attention on what he termed "good types." Schmid argued that the inherent nature of many economic goods (to include services) is a direct cause of our relationships to one another in the economic and social system. Interdependence based on physical or biological characteristics can be driven on the production side or the consumption side or may be due to the complexity of the situation such as the number and type of economics agents participating in a given situation.

The classic source of interdependence is when an economic good or service can only be consumed by one party and is only available at a positive marginal cost. This is the classic case of the private good which is both, in technical terms, a rival and low exclusion cost good or service again with a positive marginal cost. Here, we label such a good an incompatible use good.

Production-based interdependence may occur due to superordinary economies of scale all the way to marginal cost close to or equal to zero. In these cases, the interdependence created is due to the nature of the production function or the relationship between inputs and outputs. Anti-trust and utility regulation law have developed at least partially in response to the issues raised by economies of scale.

Consumption-based interdependence is another category and is generated when consumer preferences interact and influence each other. This source of interdependence is related to the potential non-rival nature of a good or service. With a non-rival good, the good (or service) can be consumed by multiple parties without exhausting the good. In technical terms, the good can enter into many utility functions without its level of availability dropping. Copyright and intellectual property law is an example of a legal field that has developed in response to non-rival goods. The law of intellectual property has developed in part to deal with the problem of non-rival goods by assessing where and to whom rights and duties should be allocated and under what conditions. Intellectual property law can be described as addressing the rights and duties related to ideas (Cwik, 2016). Ideas can be consumed by many different economic agents without reducing their existence.

Table 3.1 represents the full scope of Schmid's thoughts on interdependence via good types. Each of these represents a way in which we interact and influence each other. Economies of scale is a form of production-based interdependence; high exclusion costs, incompatibility and non-rivalry are

Table 3.1   Inherent characteristics of goods (good types)

Characteristic	Definition	Examples
High exclusion cost	A good that, if made available to Alpha, entails a high cost of excluding consumption/use by Beta. The exclusion cost is greater than net revenue.	1. Cleaner air. 2. Union benefits. Who pays? Who is a free rider? An unwilling rider?
Economies of scale	A good characterized by declining marginal cost for an additional physical unit of production.	1. Tap water. 2. Airlines. Who pays fixed cost and who pays only marginal cost?
Incompatible use	A good with two or more uses and/or users which are at odds: if Alpha (Beta) consumes/uses it for activity 1 (2), then Beta cannot consume/use it for activity 2 (1).	1. Air (between industry and breather). 2. Land (between farmer A and B).
Non-rival	A good for which there is zero marginal cost per additional use or user: one person can consume/use the good without decreasing the amount available for consumption/use by another (consumption/use is non-rival).	1. National defense (within physical boundaries). 2. Cable television.
Transaction costs	Cost of executing transaction, including cost of: • establishing a transaction position; • locating a transaction partner; • negotiating an agreement; and • monitoring and enforcing the agreement.	1. Buying/selling a home. 2. Buying/selling a car.
High information cost	A good which requires cost > 0 to measure quality of its attribute(s), beyond minimal use of the five senses. In its most extreme form, quality can only be measured/known by consumption of the good (Nelson's experience good).	1. Liability of accidents. 2. Product attributes (organic, non-genetically modified, etc.).

Source: Authors' interpretation, based on Schweikhardt (2016) and Schmid (2004).

forms of consumption-based forms of interdependence; and then there are information-based and transaction cost forms of interdependence.

A number of legal fields have developed based on the specific economic characteristics of certain industries. For example, copyright law developed to address the problem of economic goods that could be readily copied. Utility regulation law developed to address the problem of industries that had high or extraordinary economies of scale. Property law exists due to some of the unique physical characteristics of real property and our attachment to that property. Each of them is directly tied to the physical nature of some good or production type.

The production of ideas is clearly an important part of value creation in the twenty-first-century economy. When thinking about the "good type" and potential interdependence, ideas are an example where distinguishing between production and consumption-based interdependence is important. The production of ideas may be subject to economies of scale or possibly even a near-zero marginal cost. At the same time, consumers may be interdependent because of the non-rival nature of the good. These various sources of interdependence need to be kept separate in analysis as they are addressed by different institutional alternatives. The two sources of interdependence may interact and influence each other.

In some cases, the type of good may affect the analysis and in other cases it may not. A useful starting point is to determine the "good type" for the situation that is being analyzed. After that, the good type may be useful or may fall into the background and become less useful. A good type will be useful when the specific nature of the interdependence hinges on biological or physical characteristics such as a "commons" good where exclusion is difficult or a situation where the marginal cost of production tends towards zero. In other cases, these characteristics may be less important.

THINK ABOUT IT ...
Identifying Characteristics of Goods

Imagine you used the neighboring communities' outdoor, unfenced pool. There was a sign that said "gym use for community residents only." No one was around to stop you, so you used the pool without paying for it. What kind of good is it?

To answer this question, you would first need a bit more information. Imagine the gym website says that it is funded through the community's homeowner's association (HOA). In this case, use of the pool is a non-rival good with a low exclusion cost. The HOA has chosen an institutional structure that has high enforcement costs to exclude non-payers (no fence or any kind of security or check to exclude non-payers), but this does not change the characteristics of the good. It does, however, influence interdependence between the HOA (or the paying residents who do not want non-residents in their pool) and any non-resident users (you).

3.6   A HOHFELDIAN INSTITUTIONAL ANALYSIS FRAMEWORK

With these advanced topics, the analyst has the ability to begin to uncover the legal relations at play between economic agents in a given situation. In a typical economic analysis, the situation is assessed as to identifying buyers and sellers and the availability of information such as prices and quantities. With this information in hand, an analyst can turn to understanding the equilibrium and more importantly perhaps changes in that equilibrium (or comparative statics) as changes in some exogenous variable (i.e. income, consumer taxes and preferences, technology). This type of analysis can be carried out with or without the full set of data as long as the analyst has a basic understanding of the nature of the economic agents and the market involved.

The school of thought known as "law and economics" generally takes the position that economics can inform the structure of law to achieve goals such as economic efficiency and wealth maximization. For example, a certain form of liability rule would be found to maximize wealth or welfare. This approach presupposes that human behavior is relatively set and founded on rational choice and therefore law must conform to this reality.

The framework and approach to institutional impact analysis (as inspired by Hohfeld and others) presented here provides a different view on how to proceed. It is to first understand the legal foundations of the institutional situation at hand. This approach starts from the contextual foundations of the economic agents or decision makers. The interdependence should be identified as it exists between these agents and the problem that one is observing. This interdependence we observe may come from one or both of (1) the legal status quo which can be identified by the distribution of rights, duties, power and immunities amongst others that exist as a baseline and (2) biological or physical characteristics of the economic goods in the problem at hand. One or both may exist in any situation, but it is crucial to fully describe and depict the institutional situation at hand.

The analyst can then consider alternative institutional regimes that could exist to guide and structure the interdependence of the participants. The Hohfeldian language can be used in its simplest and advanced forms to understand the institutional and legal relationships among the participants. These changes should be sought from comparisons of other similar situations, alternatives from historical comparison or even new ideas of how interdependence can be addressed.

Once all the alternatives are identified including the status quo, the analyst can then assess performance. Performance will depend on the interaction between the situation and the institutional alternatives along with any conduct or behavioral assumptions (discussed later). Each institutional set of alternatives can then be examined from how wealth, income and resources are distributed under each one. The public, government officials, the judiciary and the participants themselves can become consumers of this information on the impact of alternatives.

THINK ABOUT IT ...
An LEP Example with Housing

A classic situation examined by economists is the case of housing supply and demand and the impact of rent control. Rent control, in the simple neoclassical economics model, is generally found to reduce rent due to a price ceiling while also reducing the quantity of housing available. This quantity impact is likely due to the reduced incentives for producers to bring housing units or keep existing units on the market. How does a Hohfeldian approach differ and provide insights unique to that analysis?

Let us start with a simple situation where there are housing suppliers and housing demanders (renters). We will assume a situation where "freedom of contract" exists in all dimensions as a starting point. This means that the government has placed no conditions on private housing that will be agreed upon between buyers and sellers. Of course, standard common law contract provisions still exist such as the fact that a seller cannot lie to a buyer about the condition of a property.

The imposition of a price control means that a housing rental contract now has specific provisions that will be regulated regarding the maximum price that can be placed in that contract. The Legal-Economic Performance approach to impact analysis as introduced in Chapter 4 would consider the freedom of contract situation as the first institutional alternative. The imposition of rent control (price ceiling) is the second institutional alternative. The relative question is then to determine the distribution of benefits (also assets) and costs (and liabilities) between the economic agents.

At a very basic level, the question becomes one of whether we want more housing or more income for households. There is more at stake than the outcome of this analysis, however. There is also the question of power in the economy. A law that creates a price ceiling shifts the rights and duties of the situation. At first glance, the law creates power for the tenant who is seeking shelter. A price ceiling restriction in a housing contract creates a duty on the landlords and provides a right to the tenants. The tenants have a right that the price of their dwelling shall not exceed a certain amount. However, our analysis of the distribution of legal rights and power in the housing market should not end there.

Will some types of tenants have more power than others? Will there be a distinction, for example, between high-income and low-income tenants? These are all valid questions that can be addressed through applied research and empirical analysis. This analysis might need to take place across multiple locations and time periods to understand all the dynamics involved. Again, the Hohfeldian language allows the analyst to describe the legal positions under institutional alternatives and how they may compare to one another. As with other examples, the various institutional alternatives are Pareto efficient each and non-comparable to each other.

3.7   CHAPTER RECAP

- Many legal situations including the ownership of a resource or an entitlement can be conceived of as a bundle of rights that can be separated from one another. The analyst needs to break down and consider what any situation that involves rights or property ownership means in terms of the separate pieces.
- From an institutional impact analysis standpoint, different regimes mean that the bundle will be broken down differently for various economic agents. The distribution of the bundle will have important implications for economic performance outcomes.
- Hohfeldian basic rights and duties can be combined into aggregations that are even better descriptors of jural or legal relations such as common rights, liberty and protected privilege. The analyst can use these Hohfeldian jural relations to understand an economic situation more deeply.
- Any economy includes the composition and distribution of power across various agents. Hohfeldian power is not wielded equally across the agents in an economy and ultimately the exercise of power involves coercion or the limitation of options for one or another set of agents.
- The legal remedy to enforce rights and duties is a crucial part of how the institutional alternatives have impact and consequences for agents. Part of enforcement is **the ability of one agent to receive compensation or stop the actions of another agent (or both in some cases) if a breach or damages has occurred**. The enforcement of rights or legal remedies is important as it constitutes the full scope of how the law and the legal system impact the economy and economic performance.
- In some cases, the nature of physical or biological interdependence can be important in understanding the impact of various institutional alternatives for different economic agents. This form of understanding can supplement the basic Hohfeldian model in cases where a physical or biological inter-

dependence is evident. The various characteristics that we can explore in this category include: incompatible use goods, high exclusion cost goods, economies of scale goods, transaction costs and non-rival goods.

• The full Hohfeldian economics model is based on the idea that there is more to economic decision making than budget constraints, preferences and technology. In fact, legal enablement and obligations shape economic decision making in very important ways. These legal positions can be investigated as institutional alternatives structuring the interdependence of economic agents and the impact of each alternative can be examined and compared using the Hohfeldian language.

NOTES

1. There have been numerous expansions on and modifications to Hohfeld's seminal paper. The framework has received criticism as well as spirited defense in the 100+ years since its publication. Institutional economists, including John R. Commons, Warren Samuels, A. Allan Schmid and Daniel Bromley (as well as legal scholars such as Pierre Schlag, Ted Sichelman, Matthew Kramer, Mark Andrews, Kit Barker among others), have found it useful for talking about institutions in various economic contexts.

2. McKean (1992), Bromley and Cernea (1989), Schlager and Ostrom (1992), among others, discuss the unfortunate mislabeling of common property as meaning unowned resources and the issues associated with this usage.

3. William Blackstone was an English judge and legal thinker in the eighteenth century.

4. Since the 1980s legal scholars have questioned whether some legal concepts are simply fundamental and cannot be unpacked into pieces of a bundle. At this time, there is no resolution to this debate and the bundle of rights retains much of this important analytical capacity and will be used in this text.

5. Interestingly, in all of this discussion, Honore does not mention or cite Hohfeld. Nevertheless, many legal scholars have noted and written that Hohfeld is the clear inspiration for the idea of the bundle of rights.

6. Public right of action is not a term typically used in the legal literature but is used here for a clear understanding of institutional alternatives.

4.   The Legal-Economic Performance framework

THINK ABOUT IT …

In Chapter 2, we introduced a new terminology for talking about institutional structure. How might this terminology help us describe the *Miller* (1928) case?

Both parties had the **privilege** of growing their respective trees. Prior to the ruling, each party had an equal **exposure** to the other party exercising that **privilege** (by growing their trees on their property). Once cedar rust became an issue, apple growers' **exposure to damages** from cedar growers **exercising their privilege** increased, fundamentally **changing the relationship** between cedar growers and apple growers within distance to be harmed. The court ruling maintaining the Cedar Rust Act shifted the burden the other way, **increasing exposure** of cedar growers within some distance of apple growers, and **diminishing their privilege**.

The description above should make it clear that there are physical, changing relations between the parties involved. Moreover, it captures the specifics of what individuals have – or do not have – as this conflict develops. In this chapter, we formally introduce a model of institutional impact analysis that utilizes the legal terminology developed in Chapters 2 and 3 to assist us in thinking about problems like this and beyond. The LEP framework introduced here will enable you to not only understand the shifts in interdependence noted above, but also predict these shifts under different institutional alternatives and their subsequent performance consequences.

4.1   BUILDING THE MODEL

Institutional impact analysis can tackle questions at all levels of institutions. These may range from situations at the constitutional level, like the impact of electing judges versus appointing judges, to the everyday level, such as specifics of alternate traffic codes or rules within an organization. The goal of institutional impact analysis, like in any form of impact analysis, is to predict or calculate the consequence or performance of some change in institutions as compared to the status quo.

Institutional impact analysis in particular attempts to explain how alternative institutional structures affect instances of human interdependence and substantive economic outcomes of wealth and its distribution. Institutional impact analysis begins with an institutional situation – the current environment that includes the formal and informal institutions currently in play – as well as the human conflict and cooperation taking place within it. It then considers some alternative(s) to some element of the current situation before evaluating the conduct and performance of the individuals involved in the change.

The difference in institutional impact analysis is in the emphasis on the institutional variable. There are several existing models that do this, notable among them A. Allan Schmid's SSP[1] model of institutional analysis. The model built on the paradigm first developed in industrial organization to help provide a framework for understanding the impact of "institutions" or rules of the game on economic outcomes. Where the SSP model focused on the identification of characteristics of goods or "good types" for clarifying the issue of interdependence in a specific conflict, however, the LEP framework further homes in on the issue of ubiquitous interdependence through the addition of a taxonomy of jural relations to describe and compare institutional structures as introduced in the preceding chapters.

Let us review some terminology. Conceptually, the LEP framework process looks like Figure 4.1.

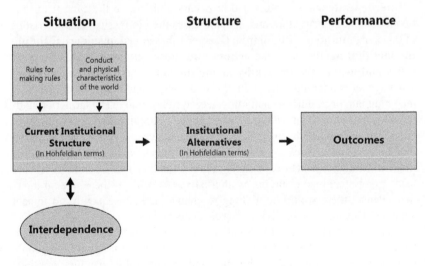

Figure 4.1   The Legal-Economic Performance framework

The **institutional situation** is about understanding the nature of interdependence between parties or actors in the economy. It means identifying how different economic actors' decisions could impact or affect one or more other parties. It also requires a deeper understanding of the existing structure of the economy including the biophysical characteristics of that world and the human-created cultural and legal rules in place at a given point in time. It includes the rules in use and the rules for making rules, which make up the current institutional structure. This crucial first step in the LEP framework is the same as in SSP and is arguably one of Schmid's most important contributions to institutional analysis. A series of unstated assumptions are typically held constant in the background, including assumptions about the nature of the interdependence forcing the search for institutional change (Klammer, Scorsone and Whalen (2021)). From there, a variety of alternatives can be explored.

The situation as specified in Schmid's SSP framework and now in the LEP model sets the stage for the rest of the analysis. Proper specification of the situational context is thus critical in ensuring the proper use of the model. The situation represents the exogenous part of the model or, in other words, the part we are not explaining. If a firm were considering a change in some corporate policy, for instance, the institutional situation would include all aspects of existing policy, and laws of the land that overtake it, as well as the current behavior (and possible changes) of those impacted or otherwise involved in the policy. This is the context that allows the researcher to properly identify interdependence at the root of the issue.

Interdependence is conditioned or occurs both due to the current institutional context and structure and in some cases the biophysical characteristics of the economic goods. Recall from Chapter 1 that **interdependence is simply the fact that parties can take actions and those actions will impact, positively and negatively, the reality facing the other parties in the situation**. The kayaker is interdependent with those municipal and industrial entities that may maintain *or* pollute the natural waterways they enjoy. The farmer or landowner is interdependent with the cattle rancher whose livestock may wander or create waste or other damage. This interdependence can prompt changes that lead one or more parties to consider or actively seek an adjustment or change in the institutional structure. Something present in this interdependence is what leads to a reimagined or proposed alternative structure. If there was no interdependence, there would be nothing to change and subsequently no impact analysis. This makes identifying interdependence key.

Both a description of the situation of interdependence and subsequent structure can be broken down into concrete legal terminology of how people relate (or are interdependent) with one another. The Hohfeldian jural relations provide the language for how we will describe the nature of interdependence and structure. In the case of a proposed change in corporate policy, for instance, we would look at the piece of policy impacted and arrange a list of those involved and each of their legal relations, before moving on to potential modifications. A better understanding of the existing rights structure might also assist in arranging the potential alternatives that might be most impactful.

The **institutional alternatives** are the proposed changes to the institutional situation. When these alternatives are examined, they can also be broken down into legal terms of who gets what. They are changes in the human-created institutions, whether rules in use or rules for making rules,[2] that are currently guiding and regulating human behavior. Institutional alternatives need to be conceived of as discrete changes in the rules. These alternatives are attempts to address situations of interdependence, resulting in outcomes of varying performance.

For instance, homeowners often have some limited rights to not have their homes searched or entered by law enforcement without a certain process being followed, such as obtaining a warrant. Policy alternatives that reduce the number of steps law enforcement must take before lawfully gaining access to a private residence reduce the duty burden of those individuals along with the homeowner's correlative rights. Some rights shift to exposure on the part of the homeowner, who now is subject to the new privileges obtained by law enforcement. Other agents in this situation might also be examined for what subsequent legal relations might be weakened or strengthened. From there, we can hypothesize or calculate what each of these means for potential performance.

Performance will depend upon realized or unrealized assumptions about human behavior or conduct including expectations and impact of enforcement changes. Each change in jural relations examined in the structural piece of the analysis has some performance consequence for the involved parties (even if that consequence is no change in x relation). These can be measured in various ways, most commonly through some estimated valuation of the lost (or gained) tradable opportunity to the agent(s), or general description of what the enablements/disablements gained or lost mean for each agent(s). Qualitative as well as quantitative metrics are useful here.

For a change in work from home policy, for instance, we might include some performance measures of increased productivity for the firm (perhaps more work completed, or fewer sick days used by workers), increased happiness for the workers (greater flexibility, less stress, etc.) or even loss of work group cohesion and camaraderie with a decrease in face-to-face time. It is important to put these measures in terms of the stakeholders they are affecting, as a result of that specific change in structure.

Situation, interdependence (or situation of interdependence), institutional alternatives and performance are what make up the Legal-Economic Performance Framework. The key takeaway is that the institutional situation informs everything downstream, except for those higher-level formal and informal institutions that are held constant (and condition the structures available). When the institutional structure – rules in use, etc. – are modified or modification is proposed, interdependence is being modified and, with it, performance. Performance is then the measure of what each party might get, assuming different levels of conduct or behavior implicit to the specific situation. In the following sections, we look at each of these pieces in detail, providing simple worked examples to help guide the process.

THINK ABOUT IT ...
What Impact Analysis Is Not

When estimating performance outcomes later on, the importance of specifying the situation and element of time in the analysis carefully becomes obvious. It would not be institutional impact analysis, for instance, to estimate performance of the apple orchardists in *Miller* (1928) before the pathogen became a problem and compare this to their performance after. That is a different kind of impact analysis, one that focuses on the impact of the physical pathogen – cedar rust – in one institutional setting rather than holding the situation constant and comparing how that setting might play out under several institutional alternatives. The performance of the apple and cedar growers under the status quo institutional arrangement before the pathogen issue became apparent is very different from the performance under that same arrangement after cedar rust rose to local attention. This difference is what gave rise to the very issue. A micro-institutional impact analysis like LEP focuses on one point in time (in this case, after the entomologist became aware of cedar rust) and looks at how that situation plays out under different institutional arrangements (i.e. a bundle of rights favoring the cedar owners versus a bundle of rights favoring the apple grower, or some mix, etc.).

Similarly, comparing the performance of an enterprise under two different types of technology would not be impact analysis. For instance, in looking at the profitability of harvesting timber residues for use in energy production, there are alternative logging techniques more appropriate for residue harvest that might have been adopted under different economic/institutional conditions than those currently used in a particular region. We could compare institutional alternatives that might impact adoption or change in the technology, such as a subsidy program for the machinery or for residue harvest, but comparing the performance of the two technologies on their own is not institutional impact analysis. For that, we might compare two different organizational policies aimed toward encouraging increased adoption or harvest, or perhaps proposed subsidy legislation, etc. Institutional impact analysis is about outlining the current situation, its institutional or legal underpinnings, and identifying the key interdependencies.

4.2   SITUATION OF INTERDEPENDENCE

Like most economic analyses, we start with the identification of some research question(s). This could range from analysis of the different proposals at the heart of a labor dispute between individuals and firms to conflicts arising from various environmental externalities and beyond.[3] This is where we identify the problem to be addressed, leading directly into the identification of the key issue(s) of interdependence.

Conflict and interdependence may originate from several sources and in several forms. In some situations, behavior may not be desirable, and some agent(s) seek to address it via a modification of institutional structure. In others, behavior may be unchanged, but now some physical change or development has occurred, such as the emergence or discovery of a new plant pathogen, a deadly virus, new technology or a change in behavior that is not covered by existing rules and laws in a way deemed to be adequate by some involved party (often because some new or increased burden has emerged). When this is the case, those good types we mentioned earlier may assist in starting the analysis and sketching the situation. In still others, there may be questions regarding existing rules that may be unclear or up for debate more explicitly.

In general, when researching an issue it is key to remember that there is *always* some kind of existing "rights" (term used generally) or network of jural relations present. It will never be an issue of assigning rights where there are none, as the economics literature is often keen to say, but rather analyzing the mixture of existing jural relations and the impacts of potential modifications as they pertain to stakeholders.

Sometimes, enforcement issues lay at the heart of a situation of interdependence, and second-level Hohfeldian legal relations must be explored. Often, these issues and those mentioned above are not mutually exclusive. What all of these have in common is a desire by some party x to structure performance outcomes more generally in the way they prefer. This means issues of power must be observed before any economizing can begin (Schmid, 2004, p. 90). We must pay attention to the questions we are not asking as much as those that we are.

The following questions are examples of topics that could be addressed using LEP:

1.   What is the impact of the allocation of alternative rights between a swimmer and a boater at a busy lake?

2. What are the structural issues involved in illegal trash dumping in a large
    city?
3. What are the interdependencies involved in the resettlement of Syrian
    refugees in the U.S. and what are the impacts of institutional alternatives
    to each of these?
4. What is the impact of mandatory helmet laws for biking in x metro versus
    the current no-law structure?
5. How might x structural changes deal with the issue of rampant product
    fraud on Amazon.com?

Notice that in each of these problem statements, we are using positive ('what')
statements rather than normative ('should') statements. The goal of impact
analysis is not to identify some correct moral answer to a question like 'Should
helmets be mandatory when biking in x location?' but rather to conduct an
analysis of the legal (or more informal) relations at play under possible institutions and their respective impacts. Yes, impact analysis of a rule requiring
helmets versus no rule might yield evidence that indicates less serious injuries
under the rule, providing a compelling point of support for the rule that you as
the researcher can then use. But the analysis itself is not the decision maker.
LEP provides information to inform choices, not make them. Choice always
involves some normative element of who or what should matter.

It should also be clear that in each of these, we are comparing some alternative structure(s) x, y, etc. to the current structure in place. Laying out the
current institutional arrangement (those rules for making rules and rules in use
mentioned earlier) is the next step in the framework. This is where you conduct
a lot of the initial grunt work on background and context. Depending on where
you are starting the analysis, you may already have all of this, or none of it.
You will want to look at the existing rules and laws surrounding your topic,
how they have been applied, the physical details such as time and place and the
scope of the issue you might want to tackle.

Many research topics, like the Syrian refugee crisis mentioned above, will
include interdependencies that could each have their own impact analysis.
Researching the issues may involve looking at existing legal precedence,
proposed legislation and related rules and interests. Whether you focus on one
angle or all will have significant consequences for the end product. In general,
added details will only simplify your work moving forward.

For instance, if we were asked to analyze the potential impact of a proposed
law at the federal level that would allow a province to ban a certain substance,
we would also have to understand and lay out existing rules that would affect
that law, such as a law that disallows that same province from spending money
to enforce the ban, or some other superseding rule that may impede a proposed
change, to conduct an effective analysis. In a situation where individuals

are illegally dumping trash on the streets of a city, creating conflict with the affected residents, it would be extremely useful to know (1) the letter of the law regarding dumping in the area including enforcement methods, (2) the context in which it was occurring (has this always been happening? Is this a new incident? What changed?) and (3) the rules, costs and structure of trash collection in the area (and maybe even surrounding areas) for both individuals and all other going concerns. In each case this first, higher institutional level defines and limits the set of practical forms of economic organization available to economic actors in the next step.[4] This information frames your analysis going forward (though you will likely add to it as you go).

As we learned in our review of A. Alan Schmid's work, the biological and physical characteristics of the interdependence between the parties or agents can be part of the institutional situation. In some cases, the biophysical nature of the economic good under consideration is an important part of the analysis. The same economic good may express different characteristics depending on the exact interaction between parties. For example, air quality has the characteristic of an incompatible use between parties. A factory owner may wish to use the air above the factory as a sink for production residuals while the residents who live near the factory may wish to use the air for breathing. The air can either be clean or dirty or somewhere in between but it is a discrete choice; the air cannot be both. There are also cases, however, where the nature of the economic good may be less important in understanding institutional situations. In conducting an ex post impact analysis of a court decision, for instance, knowing that the decision is incompatible is obvious and adds little to the discussion. Recognizing that a particular situation revolves around a good where the marginal cost of another use or user is zero, however, might help guide the kinds of alternatives that are compared to those of different relevant pricing structures.

4.2.1   Identifying Key Interdependence

It is not always obvious where the true issue of interdependence lies. Thinking about how the existing institutional situation has created the conflict in question helps get at the heart of interdependence. Interdependence **always** occurs *between* individuals or parties, and there are often multiple parties/ interdependencies present. Identifying the situation and the correct parties to the interdependence in question is key to properly setting up the model.

The analyst should also consider the interaction of several collective entities or going concerns (such as between the state and some industry or industry and union, etc.) and there will be rules that will direct the conflict that may exist between them. For instance, a dispute over a piece of land can have interdependencies between neighbor A and neighbor B as well as interdependencies between a neighbor and the land surveyor (who A might agree with and B might not). The same dispute can also create an interdependence between neighbor B and a judge who decides the dispute in favor of neighbor A, or neighbor B and those involved in a convoluted appeals process. These rules give clues as to the interdependence present. Properly specifying and understanding this interdependence and where it is coming from is key to a successful impact analysis.

Consider an example. Suppose that there is a situation where a market has a large surplus of grain or some other agricultural crop. Agriculture lobbyists in a neighboring developing country petition for the government to raise trade tariffs on the country of surplus so that they may protect against disruptions to their own domestic grain market as a result of potential below-market dumping of the product. An independent analyst is asked to conduct an impact analysis of various versions of their proposed change. Where does the analyst start?

Following the interdependence methodology outlined here, the analyst would start by looking at existing laws and rules impacting the particular tariff that the lobbyists are seeking to increase (such as whether and how it can be changed and time considerations, etc.), laws regarding the dumping of the product in both the U.S. and the developing country, as well as more basic pro-cedural rules for how a lobbying group can be involved in the process. More physical information such as size of surplus, conditions of markets and prices in both countries, size of tariff or similar tariffs, etc. would also be gathered. The analyst would identify all the relevant parties involved – the farmers (in both locales!), the lobbyists, the government (or rule-making body involved) and those involved or impacted by changes in the tariff in the developing country – and would be able to identify the key issue of interdependence. In this case, interdependence is centered around export pricing for foreign grain: U.S. farmers want export costs to be as low as possible (to maximize profits), and those opposed (in this case likely for various reasons, dumping concerns and international relations among them) want them at some level greater than present. With information regarding the situation (background rules and laws) and a firm understanding of the conflict at hand (tariff pricing), the analyst can then specify the institutional alternatives available (tariff increase versus no change; any other institutional alternatives) and the potential performance implications for the interdependent parties.

We work through two different examples below to demonstrate this process. Example 4.1 is without the use of Hohfeld language of jural relations. Example 4.2 uses the Hohfeldian language more formally to highlight how it can also be helpful to outline the initial situation of interdependence. For now, focus on understanding the situation and the interdependence parts of the model. We will cover structure in more detail as well as the performance piece with examples of each in Sections 4.3. and 4.4.

Example 4.1
Think about a situation in which the state has a law that permits cities to tax homeowners on up to 50 percent of their home's value annually. An assessor in a city in that state, say called Quibbletown, decides the value of the home based on an algorithm that the city's tax assessors have followed for decades. During this time, the economic climate of the city has deteriorated dramatically, severely impacting the market valuation of homes in Quibbletown's downtown area. Yet, the city's valuation of those properties has remained roughly the same, resulting in property taxes that many in the downtown area feel are unfairly high.

The analyst has been given the task of assessing this situation and providing possible solutions or ways forward for the city (Table 4.1). To begin the analysis, further background information is collected. Then, the analyst can start thinking about all the interdependent parties and what each is concerned with. This could include the process of talking to individuals familiar with the situation and reviewing the law and how similar conflicts like this have been addressed (or not). These are some of the additional details:

1. The taxpayers may challenge the assessor's valuation of their home if they can provide proof of a conflicting valuation. The law is vague as to what this proof might be, but generally acceptable forms seem to include a letter of assessment from another independent certified assessor. This proof must be given within a relatively short window of time.
2. The town's tax assessor can decline to modify the valuation. They have been doing so, often with no reason given.
3. If the town assessor does not agree to lower the valuation to what the taxpayer considers reasonable, there are further opportunities to appeal the decision, but these opportunities are increasingly time consuming and costly to the individual.

In this situation, we have numerous parties involved: state and local lawmakers, the city, taxpayers, assessors and others involved in the valuation and tax process. What key interdependence lies at the heart of this situation?
Since all details of the situation point to issues regarding property valuation, we can sense that the valuation itself is the primary issue to be sorted out. The key interdependence here is the disagreement between the taxpayer and the assessor as to the real value of the property. The institutions that structure or guide this interdependence are the state laws and local rules, as well as any professional code for assessors, that shape the town's assessing process. While lawmakers, and the 50 percent rule they implemented, are involved in creating this situation, they are part of the overarching institutional structure that is held constant for this analysis. The city itself has a relationship with both the

Table 4.1   Fair housing valuation in Quibbletown

Situation	Interdependence (parties/structure)	
Homes in Quibbletown can be taxed on up to 50 percent their last assessed value. Assessors use an algorithm that is not tied to market value. Homeowners feel they are being taxed unfairly, with homes assessed well above market value by city assessors. They can challenge assessment, but this can be costly and city assessors can reject (and they often do).	Between the homeowner v city assessors (operating on behalf of the city).	Homeowners must pay (have liability?) taxes on up to 50 percent of the value of the home, as determined by city assessors. Assessors must provide a fair assessment of the home value. The homeowner has the right to appeal. The assessor has a duty to review the appeal and the privilege to reject it. *How is "fair value" determined?*

Note: Once all the details have been laid out, the analyst then utilizes the Hohfeldian framework to map out the current rights and duties at play. This then could provide a starting place for a comparison of other institutional alternatives that might move or adjust the value of those jural relations. In this case, the town assessor has the Hohfeldian power to set property valuations which are a Hohfeldian liability to the property owners. This power was conferred by the state legislative body and any local ordinances. The exercise of this power will then create a duty to pay the tax liability on the property owner. The failure to pay taxes could trigger a secondary Hohfeldian relation related to the power of the tax assessor to certify this problem to another legal body. The property owner has been conferred with a Hohfeldian power to appeal the valuation through the proper channels. This is a compound power because it can be sued with more than one appeal body. This exercise of power of course comes with the opportunity costs that must be factored into the property owner's decision-making process. The specific nature of the property owner's power in this process can drive how large and extensive those opportunity costs are and in a sense represents a form of the mutual coercion we discussed earlier. A more burdensome process can foreclose options for the property owners and distribute wealth and resources in a different manner.

assessors (who work for the city) and the taxpayers (who live in the city) but leaves the responsibility of calculating a legal property tax to the assessors. The assessors are responsible for the valuation, the heart of our analysis, and the taxpayers are the ones disputing it. One of the key interdependencies is that between the taxpayer and the assessor, over the valuation (or "reasonable valuation") itself. The outcome of the assessing process is an important driver in a number of economic performance variables including the distribution of wealth in neighborhoods, the shaping of local housing and property investment decisions and the distribution of income between the public and private sector.

The work done in these first stages helps inform the questions that may emerge, or the true issue of interdependence. In this case, we can see that there is some conflict over what qualifies as a fair valuation, as well as the process behind this that is informing interdependence between the homeowners and the assessors who are operating on behalf of the city. Clarifying this piece of the process – how valuation is fairly determined – will effectively determine which stakeholder faces the greater burden. Of course, identifying the true source of interdependence in a scenario is not always so straightforward. In some situations, legal remedy will play a much more prominent role, signaling the need for a second-level Hohfeldian analysis. Example 4.3 works through one such case.

Interdependence is clarified by identifying the set of independent variables that make up the environment, or the situation of interdependence. These include existing embedded institutions, habits and other aspects of the physical world that condition or create the interdependence. Interdependence may come from the physical and biological characteristics of the situation and the goods and services involved or from the nature of the institutions (rules) currently in place. The specifics of the situation of interdependence in question set the foundation for the rest of the analysis.

Once the interdependence is identified, different structures for sorting it out can be considered. From there, the performance of these structural alternatives (or their impact on the situation of interdependence) can be evaluated. Bringing in elements of legal analysis to outline institutional situations and structures in terms of rights (and duties), as discussed in Section 4.3, will further clarify these issues.

4.3 ALTERNATIVE STRUCTURE

It should now be clear that defining institutional structure is necessary for both (1) laying out the situation and interdependence and (2) identifying the possible options for addressing the interdependence in question. The **structure** is the independent variable of the analysis. This is comprised of the institutional alternatives that are available, holding the institutional situation, including the current rules for making rules or other higher-level institutions, constant.

As discussed above, the attributes of the institutional situation inform the interdependence – but it also simultaneously defines the institutional alternatives available. For instance, background laws might inform potential avenues for dealing with interdependence, such as rules against seeking vigilante justice, or steps for petitioning a local community or government to change a particular rule or law, etc. The characteristics of the goods in question, also part of that institutional situation that is held constant, similarly inform the viable structural alternatives that are available.

Not all alternatives available will necessarily be applicable to the work you are doing. Often, institutional impact analysis involves analyzing one other

Table 4.2   Jural correlatives

Entitlements	Disablements
Right: A claim that Beta must do or not do something in relation to Alpha	Duty: The other end of a right. An obligation that Beta must do or not do something in relation to Alpha
Privilege: Ability of Alpha to act in a certain manner without being held liable for damages to others (Beta(s))	Exposure: Beta is subject to damages from Alpha's actions without legal remedy
Power: Alpha's ability to change their legal relationship with Beta	Liability: Beta's relationship to Alpha is susceptible to being changed
Immunity: Beta's relations to Alpha cannot be legally altered by Alpha	Disability: Alpha is unable to change their legal relationship with Beta

possible institutional alternative against the status quo institution, though others may exist. Other times, you might be comparing two new alternatives.

As in framing the situation and interdependence, specificity is key to defining institutional structure and alternatives. To that end, this part of the analysis heavily utilizes the Hohfeld language of legal relations introduced in Chapter 2 and expanded further in Chapter 3. Refer to Table 4.2 for a review of the basic jural relations.

Let us consider an example of alternative structures regarding right of way at a local lake in Everytown, U.S.

Example 4.2
In April, an incident involving an operator of a small speed boat resulted in a swimmer being hospitalized. The incident occurred at a busy local beach during daylight hours after the operator had been drinking on his boat after a long day of work. In this incident, the driver's boat was damaged, and the swimmer was hospitalized with serious injuries. Assuming there are no existing written rules for this scenario, analyze the potential institutional structures.

In Table 4.3, we see a few different institutional hypotheticals that could play out. If it is determined that the swimmer has the right of way, and the boater holds the corresponding duty of non-interference, then we can imagine things will go poorly for the boater upon striking the swimmer. If hit while in the water, the swimmer or their estate can claim damages and injury in a court of law.

If the boater is deemed to have the right of way, then the swimmer may be out of luck. Likely, this latter scenario sounds ridiculous to most readers. Realistically, the boater is likely to have some kind of limited-use right to use the lake and his boat in a way deemed to be responsible (not drunk, within

Table 4.3   Structural alternatives of lake use

	LEP analysis matrix
Situation	**Structural alternatives**
A swimmer at a lake in Everytown,	*Alternative 1*
U.S. was struck by a drunk	Swimmer has the use right to the lake. Boater has the duty of
speed-boater	non-interference
Interdependence	*Alternative 2*
Swimmer wants to safely swim. Boater	Boater has the use right to the lake. Swimmer has the duty of
wants to drink and boat. Their uses are	non-interference
incompatible in this instance	*Alternative 3*
	Boater has the limited-use right to drive his boat responsibly
	on the lake and Swimmer has the limited-use right to swim
	responsibly on the lake in a designated beach area. Both have
	corresponding duties of (reasonable) non-interference

some specific confines away from the shore, etc.), and the swimmer likely has some limited-use right as well to swim with care.

Both have a corresponding duty to the other party to look out and be aware. The confines of these limited rights and what is considered reasonable in these cases are likely to be trickier and determined through the legal process. In this way, understanding Hohfeldian legal relations *does not* tell you exactly what is going to happen or how performance will play out, but rather gives you some idea of possibilities to guide in your own analysis. You must still do the work of understanding relevant human behavior and collecting data, evidence and developing potential testable hypotheses (covered in Section 4.4).

What should be clear in the above is that under some institutional structures, the swimmer has more to lose than the boater. In others, the boater has more to lose. U.S. law in this case tries to balance the two interests as in alternative 3, but each party is still susceptible to these shifting jural relations.

None of these alternatives says anything about enforcement. Rather, enforcement is assumed. This is an important behavioral assumption with far-reaching consequences. In Example 4.3, we discuss the second-level Hohfeldian analysis involving enforcement issues in the case of illegal trash dumping in an older, industrial city.

Example 4.3: Trash dumping
Illegal trash dumping is a common problem in many older, industrial cities. The large amount of vacant land in former factory spaces creates the ability for illegal dumpers to free ride and use this vacant land as a dump site as opposed to using a regulated trash bin. Many of the residents do not like, or in the language of economics, do not prefer to consume a landscape filled with trash as opposed to consuming a clean and unbridled landscape near them. The

Table 4.4   Interdependence of trash dumping on city streets

Problem/Situation	Interdependence (Parties/current structure)	
Trash dumping has become an issue for residents of an older, industrial city who want a clean city	Between … Dumpers v. non-dumpers	Dumpers have duty not to dump. Non-dumpers have right to clean streets (with city enforcement)
A local law exists that makes it a misdemeanor (with fine) to dump trash	City enforcers v. dumpers	**Enforcement issues indicate second-level Hohfeldian analysis**
Currently there is not enough monitoring to catch dumpers	City enforcers v. non-dumpers	Non-dumpers do not have the power to bring action against dumpers over breached duty but must rely on local law enforcement using their Hohfeldian power
City residents are billed for trash removal via taxes		Since dumpers are unidentified, legal action is also unlikely until perpetrators are identified (**another indicator of Hohfeldian enforcement issue**)

trash dumpers prefer to consume the vacant land for their waste. An interdependence and conflict exist between those who wish to consume vacant land for trash dumping and those who wish a clean and "trashless" view (Table 4.4).

There is an existing or status quo legal and institutional structure given this interdependence. A local law exists that makes it a misdemeanor offense (with an attached fine and jail time) to dump trash outside of city-certified trash bins. That law is enforced by local police. The law gives a Hohfeldian right to city residents who seek to consume a "trashless" landscape and a Hohfeldian duty on those who are dumping. In a secondary jural relations sense, local law enforcement holds a Hohfeldian power that can be exercised to change legal relations with a suspected trash dumper. Local citizens do not hold a Hohfeldian power in this case.

The interdependence in this situation can be conceived of as between dumpers and non-dumpers and a secondary jural relationship between dumpers and the power of local law enforcement to remedy damages done to non-dumpers. Here, we can observe that the issue of secondary Hohfeldian relations and the ability to exercise a power becomes a crucial issue to investigate. The problem for local law enforcement is that the high exclusion cost nature of vacant land and lack of resources means this power is not easily exercised and results in large amounts of trash-dumping behavior going undetected. In the case of trash dumping in this city, the lack of reasonable ability for the residents of the area to hold the rule-breaking dumpers to account has created what is essentially an empty right.

Enforcement is often difficult and costly in these types of high exclusion cost scenarios, where the rule breakers are difficult to identify or charge. However, while enforcement issues are part of the second-level analysis used to identify and describe interdependence, the presence of enforcement issues does not imply that resolving enforcement is the necessary fix when it comes to possible alternative institutional structures. Rather, enforcement issues can be a good indicator of the presence of poorly defined jural relations or a structure that may need to be modified. In this case, it would be useful to know whether enforcement worked in the past and the conditions that had changed since in determining possible ways forward. In Table 4.5, we build on our existing analysis and consider some of the possible alternatives. We also consider some likely performance questions for each alternative.

The first potential structure to consider is the status quo. The status quo maintains the current mix of jural relations. It does *not* always mean the continuation of the current performance. If there are some variables of human behavior that are likely to change, bringing about a decrease in dumping behavior, this might be something considered in Section 4.4. Nevertheless, the rights/duties mix will remain the same.

In option 2, we see the current jural relations are restructured with the addition of funds to local law enforcement. This change is based on increasing funds for local law enforcement which increases their ability to exercise a Hohfeldian power in catching illegal dumpers. Here, we can observe that Hohfeldian jural relations can be expanded or contracted in a sense with resource additions or subtractions. This is especially important in the case of understanding the issue of secondary Hohfeldian jural relations related to the enforcement of existing rights and duties. This option represents a shift between dumpers and local law enforcement whereby local law enforcement's opportunity set would expand and dumpers would be more restricted.

In the third option, we see a clearer modification of existing jural relations. With the formation of a community enforcement system, depending on the way it is set up and the rules organizing it, residents now have the privilege to monitor for trash dumping combined with the Hohfeldian power to engage in enforcement via civil courts. These changes, tied with behavior, could have many different impacts on performance. We consider questions of performance and potential methods of measurement and discussion in Section 4.4, building on some prior examples as well as new scenarios.

4.4 PERFORMANCE

The final level of impact analysis attempts to explain how alternative internal structures of going concerns and contractual arrangements affect **performance**. This is the dependent variable of impact analysis and can be measured via many methods. Often, economists are asked to measure benefits and costs. This is the process for laying out performance in the LEP framework as well,

Table 4.5   *LEP framework: Trash dumping on city streets*

Problem/situation	Interdependence (parties/current structure)	Structure	Performance questions
Trash dumping in city Trash dumping has become an issue for city residents who want a clean city	Between ... Dumpers v. non-dumpers City enforcers v. dumpers	Dumpers have duty not to dump. Non-dumpers have right to clean streets (with city enforcement) **Enforcement issue indicates second-level Hohfeldian analysis**	1. Maintain current structure (status quo)
A local law exists that makes it a misdemeanor (with fine) to dump trash		Non-dumpers have the power to bring action against dumpers over breached duty (their inalienable entitlement to clean streets). This is costly, however, creating what is essentially an **empty right.**	2. Allocate increased enforcement funding to police expanding their Hohfeldian power for monitoring
Currently there is not enough monitoring to catch dumpers City residents are billed for trash removal via taxes		Since dumpers are unidentified, legal action is also unlikely until perpetrators are identified (**Another indicator of Hohfeldian enforcement issue**)	3. Establishment of community and property owner power to sue over trash dumping outside of registered city bins
			1. Non-dumpers must bear cost/risk of self-enforcement or deal with dirty streets. Dumpers continue dumping. 2. May increase enforcement; may not. Higher taxes for residents? 3. Higher cost to residents? Time? Probably less dumping

though we place added emphasis on what impact changes in jural relations in particular have on performance.

Once the alternative institutions are carefully specified, institutional analysis is not limited to any particular method of investigation. Schmid (2004) gives examples of four broad categories of empirical research: experiments, case studies, econometrics and simulation (Schmid, 2004).[5] Any of the tools used in economics might be relevant. It is up to the researcher to choose which option or options are best suited to the attributes of the case at hand.

Measures of performance might include the measurement and enforcement of implementation and other transaction costs, some valuation of gains in knowledge, social cohesion or various measures of productivity within a going concern, or measures of compliance with a rule or its adoption. If one of the institutional structures being compared is currently in place, then contrasting its performance with that expected with a different structure is an analysis of the probable consequences of change (Schmid, 2004). This says nothing about how to put the alternative in place. Comparing the consequences of a hypothetical change is very different from institutional change analysis, which is beyond the scope of this text.

In addition to the method of measurement, there are two other issues to consider. The first involves the behavioral assumptions to be made. When situation and structure are put together, some model of human behavior is needed. An external (to the agent) rule change alters the pattern of reinforcers coming from the environment and alters the probability of repetition of behavior. In some methods, such as case studies, behavior may be observed and measurable. In others, agents' conduct may be assumed. LEP regards profit maximization as one information-processing possibility from among many. The chosen model may be cost minimization, utility maximization, some model from evolutionary psychology, organizational business or economics and political economy, or some more recent theory yet to be established.

The second issue involves considering, again, what a change in legal relations means for stakeholders. One thing to note when outlining the changes in legal relations is that legal entitlements gained or lost are not themselves a performance outcome, but rather a vehicle that, when paired with conduct (and other details of the situation), leads to performance outcomes (benefits and costs). This is important in grasping distributional outcomes that matter, rather than attaching subjective weight to "rights gained" or "freedom lost" – terms we now know have transient or ambiguous meaning. Gaining a right, power or privilege, etc. are not themselves to be counted on the benefit side of the performance balance sheet, but rather the expanded opportunities they may present (gained utility or lost utility; greater flexibility in negotiating resulting in lower costs; some other valuation of future options gained, etc.) or loss of opportunity they present are what is counted. Unenforceable or similarly broken laws or rules are good examples of why performance is focused strictly on outcomes of structure and not the structure itself. For instance, a new bill may reaffirm or assert a child's right to education free of charge in their county (with the corresponding duty for the locale to provide) but depending on the specifics of that duty and corresponding right, outcomes for the student can vary widely. If the locale's duty is only to provide a building and a teacher that can reasonably house all the children in the area, but nothing about quality (or, indeed, how that "quality" is to be measured or enforced), a right may indeed have been gained, but the performance of that right could be anywhere from a poor, crowded school with an overworked teacher and dubious educational outcomes to high-quality facilities and education well beyond the letter of the law. That new "right to education" may be as empty or as full as the subsequent actions of the people who apply it.

Hypothesis testing might be used to help design the analysis to get at the performance issues of interest. Some researchers start their analyses having already formed a set of testable hypotheses. Others gather all relevant information first, then proceed to formulate and revise. Hypothesis testing provides yet another avenue for organizing your impact analysis.

Various aspects of the above example can be restated into tests, with both a null and alternative hypothesis. Hypotheses could be stated in terms of Hohfeldian jural relations or more broadly to start.

For instance:

H1: The new education bill will not change learning outcomes for students in x locale(s).

H2: The new education bill will change learning outcomes for students in x locale(s).

Testing these would require some metric for the current average level of "learning," whether that is some average test score, etc. Institutional alternatives would be tested to see if there were significant deviations from the former. In cases where the new rule has not yet been enacted, the researcher will have to produce some sort of estimate. In cases where the change has already occurred and data are available, the task of conducting these tests becomes much more straightforward.

Consider again the example of the swimmer and boater from Everytown, U.S., now with additional performance outcomes considered (Table 4.6).

What might an expansion of the performance piece of the analysis look like? We might consider drawing some hypotheses based on a change in the rule from either alternative 1 or 2 to alternative 3, based on our predicted likelihood of future incidents occurring:

Table 4.6   *LEP framework: Lake use*

LEP analysis matrix		
Situation	**Structural alternatives**	**Performance**
A swimmer at a lake in Everytown, U.S. was struck by a boater *Interdependence* Swimmer wants to enjoy and safely swim. Boater wants to use water for their enjoyment. Their uses are potentially incompatible in this instance	*Alternative 1* Swimmer has the use right to the lake. Boater has the duty of non-interference *Alternative 2* Boater has the use right to the lake. Swimmer has the duty of non-interference *Alternative 3* Boater has the limited-use right to drive his boat responsibly on the lake and Swimmer has the limited-use right to swim responsibly on the lake in a designated beach area	*Performance 1* Swimmer has the right to use the lake if Boater's bid is less than Swimmer's reservation price. Boater is liable for all damages If Boater's bid is greater than Swimmer's reservation price, Boater gains the right, Swimmer gains the liability *Performance 2* Boater has the right to drive on the lake drunk if Swimmer's bid is less than Boater's reservation price. Swimmer is liable for all damages If Swimmer's bid is greater than Boater's reservation price, Swimmer gains the right, Boater gains the liability *Performance 3* If Boater violates the conditions of the limited-use rule, then Boater is held liable for Swimmer's damages and vice versa

H1: The establishment of limited-use rights will not change incident rates on the lake.

H2: The establishment of limited-use rights will decrease incident rates on the lake.

Performance might then be reported in terms of gathered data on the number of incidents on the lake or perhaps comparison to data from a similar area with a similar rule change. Other potential performance measures might include changes in the number of users of the space, the makeup of the user groups (more boaters or more swimmers), various surveys, etc.

The above example gives a very simplified version of how the LEP model might be applied in full to the issue of rights and performance. These are not the only alternatives that might be considered, nor is this way of describing performance necessarily complete. Like any form of analysis, the analyst in effect chooses which questions to ask, which structural alternatives to consider and the way in which performance may be evaluated. The analyst decides where to start the analysis and when – with consequences for performance measurements and how they may be compared.

4.4.1   Estimating Conduct

Behavior – or conduct – drives performance. To understand performance under alternative institutional options, a model of human behavior must be considered. This is the conduct part of the LEP model. We must specify a version of human behavior (rational choice, altruism or somewhere in between) that will drive how people view the interdependence and their responses to the various institutional options. The interaction between institutional options and human behavior is the engine that drives the model toward various performance characteristics. As noted by Schmid, "The fundamental implications of bounded rationality and other tendencies of the brain suggest a world marked by fragile equilibrium or disequilibrium, necessarily incomplete markets, and where competition may not have the expected results" (Schmid, 2004, chapter 3).

Depending on the specifics of the situation/details of the case and past scenarios like it, the analyst is likely to have some idea of possible conduct of stakeholders going forward. Accurately predicting consumer behavior is incredibly important for all forms of business, to name one obvious area. It might mean the difference between loyal customers sticking with a brand when they have to cut a few corners versus losing the dissatisfied customer base to a near competitor. It might also mean losing out on sales due to a management decision that had nothing to do with the product itself but failing to anticipate how it might impact consumer perception of the brand. Regardless of the situation, the focus should remain on being explicit about assumptions being used to predict performance outcomes.

Consider the following example of the massive online retailer and marketplace, Amazon.

Example 4.4
Like many massive online marketplaces that rely on third-party sellers to sustain the breadth of product listings and availability on their platform, Amazon suffers from the issues of product quality verification. Amazon has millions of sellers, many of which are not original manufacturers, that can add products to existing listings and offer fulfillment by Amazon (Chow, 2019). Once a product listing is available, Amazon may source from numerous sellers including third-party vendors of branded products. This product is then combined from multiple sources into the supply in Amazon warehouses (Chow, 2019). This can lead customers (and product rights holders) to have a difficult time identifying the true origin of the product and in many cases the product's

legitimacy. Most consumers rely on reviews for information regarding product quality, which can have their own issues such as self-selection bias (Li and Hitt, 2008; Bjering et al., 2015) and manipulation (Hu et al., 2012). Moreover, spending time wading through these reviews and attempting to gather information in general comes with its own costs and trade-offs, and there is no way for a consumer to determine when a review is given for a legitimate product or a faulty or counterfeit version co-mingled with the warehouse supply.

Amazon under current legal structures has limited responsibility for fraudulent products and sellers. As an intermediary, Amazon is protected under the U.S. Digital Millennium Copyright Act (DCMA) so long as it complies with the "notice and takedown" procedures outlined to remove infringing products from the marketplace. The burden often falls on the rights holder (the producer) or their agent to identify infringement and then file intellectual property (IP) rights violation complaints to Amazon directly. Chow (2019) identifies what they refer to as three major enforcement problems cited often by brand owners: (1) counterfeiters use false identities and addresses and thus are untraceable; (2) brand owners must suffer through the use of cumbersome and ineffective notice and takedown procedures; and (3) existing measures used by e-commerce platforms do not deter repeat infringing activity.

Consider the interdependence present between consumers (who want the product reflected in the listings) and Amazon (who wants to maximize profit). The key issue of interdependence is over product quality verification. Both Amazon and the consumer face this issue – the structural alternatives will help determine performance and who ultimately bears the relative burden and advantages of this high information cost issue (Table 4.7).

Under the current institutional arrangement, Amazon is privileged to host product listings and not obligated (not under Hohfeldian duty) to verify product quality under the DCMA. This privilege, however, ends when their duty to not knowingly host counterfeit products begins (when an IP rights holder or agent notifies them). Consumers and IP holders are exposed to Amazon's privilege. In the case of the rights holders, the exposure falls on them up to the point that they identify fraudulent products and notify Amazon, at which point they have a right to have their IP protected (and Amazon must follow through on their duty not to interfere). In the case of consumers, they are exposed to the associated costs of vetting products on their own and potentially purchasing and using a fraudulent product.

There are three different hypothetical institutional structures considered here. Under the first, the status quo continues, as detailed above. Depending on behavioral assumptions, this could have different consequences for Amazon's bottom line. If consumers largely continue to buy products and the issue does not lead to brand deterioration (perhaps due to a generous return policy), Amazon will continue following the DCMA as required at the point where

Table 4.7 LEP framework: Product quality verification on Amazon

Problem/situation	Interdependence (parties/current structure)	Structure	Performance questions
Product fraud on Amazon Consumers increasingly report issues of fraudulent products sold via Amazon. Consumers can return products for any reason within a period, but have no way of verifying the legitimacy of the product besides what is present on the listing.	Amazon v. consumers Amazon v. sellers Amazon v. rights holders Consumers v. intellectual property rights holders	Existing rules make it such that Amazon is privileged to sell and largely exempt from duty to verify the legitimacy of products from third-party sellers (or those shipped by Amazon) under DCMA. Consumers have exposure to Amazon's sale of potential fake products. They do not have a right to a guaranteed product in this context.	1. Maintain current structure. 2. "Direct from manufacturer" labeling for goods shipped directly from manufacturer. 3. Amazon gains duty to verify legitimacy with new/expanded fines/penalties when caught selling illegitimate products.	1. Consumers bear risk (and cost) of trusting Amazon/buying or using illegitimate product. Amazon may lose profits over lost consumer base for some products. Consumers may pay more to get verified product directly from the manufacturer or elsewhere. 2. Higher costs for Amazon/potential lost efficiencies. Higher consumer trust/maintained loyalty for some products. 3. Will depend on level of fine and enforcement options. If too low, ineffective. Status quo continues (see performance above).

profits are maximized. If fraudulent listings and returns begin cutting into the bottom line, Amazon will likely act at that point to modify internal policy regarding listings. IP rights holders will bear the cost of enforcing their claims by notifying Amazon and monitoring takedown of fraudulent listings. Consumers will similarly bear the costs of vetting products as they are able (which is difficult) and will have to deal with the fall-out of faulty products and any subsequent return process or follow-up with manufacturers that could be fruitless should a fraudulent product cause serious harm.

Under the second alternative, Amazon adopts a new labeling system that indicates a level of vetting beyond the requirements of the DCMA. This does not in any way change the current distribution of jural relations from what they were under the status quo *except* for the newly labeled "Direct from Manufacturer" products. Amazon still retains the privilege to sell items limited only by the duty to comply with "notice and takedown" under the DCMA. The other parties are still exposed to this. But now consumers have a right to a vetted product on these listings and Amazon a duty to vet. This alternative might have several performance outcomes for Amazon, depending on behavioral assumptions. A Direct from Manufacturer option would disrupt Amazon's current supply chain organization and might result in lost cost efficiencies for Amazon. These costs could be passed on to the consumer (who may or may not be willing to pay more). The move might also benefit Amazon through brand image, and perhaps getting ahead of future legal issues that might arise from increasing fraudulent product claims. Or the move could deteriorate the general image of the Amazon marketplace with consumers viewing those listings without a label as inherently unsafe. Amazon also retains the Hohfeldian power to do away with this labeling system or change what it promises altogether.

The third structure increases Amazon's duty to vet products sold on the marketplace (likely through some new law or modification to the DCMA). This strengthens the corresponding rights of both the IP holders and the consumers as described under the status quo. If they do not perform their duty, they will be fined. The level of this fine or penalty and conditions of enforcement will impact performance greatly. If the fine is high, Amazon will only sell thoroughly vetted products (and listings will likely be restricted greatly as a result). If it is too low, Amazon may continue much as it has been. Some of these costs could be passed on to the consumer. Who bears enforcement costs would also play heavily into the performance outcomes of this scenario. Consumer confidence in product quality will likely be higher than under the status quo. The specifics of how this ruling is designed will greatly affect behavioral expectations and performance.

Conduct and performance could be further built out using other methods as well. Albert Hirschman's *Exit, Voice, and Loyalty* (1970) famously introduced a matrix for consumer decision making in the face of deteriorating product quality that could easily be applied as a behavioral model for predicting potential performance. If Amazon assumes consumers are likely to have some degree of brand loyalty to Amazon, regardless of whether they are vocal about their concerns or not, their predicted cost of maintaining the status quo will be lower than if loyalty is low and consumers chose to take their business elsewhere. If consumers are very vocal, be it through reviews or other social media, this might also increase some costs for Amazon (or it might not). Hirschman's model is just one example of how behavioral elements could be brought into play.

The Amazon example could be empirically examined using comparative data from several countries if the rules differ for online sellers in a global context. The key independent variable would be the varying institutional structures that would likely be some form of a discrete variable. The dependent variable might be related to economic performance such as the relative price paid for similar products in different countries that could be associated with consumer welfare.

Consider another example. Consumer behavior in light of different structures of waiter wages and tipping would also have large performance implications. In Example 4.5, we consider how wage structures for restaurant workers and subsequent conduct of patrons might impact performance.

Example 4.5
Consider two different alternatives to the existing tipping structure in a certain municipality in Michigan. Assume for the sake of this exercise that existing higher-level rules allow these alternatives to be put forward.

1. An automatic gratuity (to be paid to the waiter) of 20 percent is required in sit-down restaurants.
2. Waiters receive the same minimum wage as non-tipped employees as a baseline (in addition to tips).

When starting to outline the institutional situation, we seek to identify key interdependence. In the case of tipping dynamics in Michigan, the first two proposed alternatives are dealing with the same economic performance issue: wages for waiters in Michigan restaurants and who pays them. A bit of background research explains why these are both issues: in Michigan, an employer of a tipped employee is only required to pay $3.67 per hour (38 percent of full minimum wage) in direct wages if that amount combined with the tips received at least equals the full minimum wage of $9.65 (U.S. Department of Labor, 2021). In (1), the patrons would make up more of the difference in wages (through required tips). In (2) the owners would be responsible for the full

Table 4.8   LEP framework: Michigan waiter wage structure

Problem/ situation	Interdependence (parties/current structure)		Structure	Performance questions
Wage structure for Michigan waiters (tipped employees): patrons not required to tip; owners required to make up lost tips up to minimum wage. Waiters keep any overage once tips meet minimum, but not guaranteed any more than minimum wage if tips < difference	Waiters v. patrons	Patrons have the privilege to tip (or not). Waiters have exposure to their choice (to tip or not)	Tipping rule (automatic gratuity) Patrons have duty to tip x amount. Waiters have right to be tipped x amount regardless of service.	How will these changes impact restaurant goers (and their conduct)? How will this change waiter take-home pay? How will this change the difference in wage owners must pay?
	Waiters v. owners	Owners have a duty to make up the difference in minimum wage if not made in tips. Waiters have right to the full $9.65	Owner no longer exposed to full patron privilege to tip or not, but still subject to duty to waiter for the difference in wages Change in minimum wage baseline for waiters.	What are the cost burdens for those involved?
	Owners v. patrons	Owner exposed to patron privilege to tip or not	Patrons still have the privilege to tip (or not). Waiters still exposed to their choice. Owners have duty to pay $9.65 to waiters	

minimum wage, regardless of tipping behavior. Table 4.8 provides a general outline of what this might look like.

LEP clearly captures the performance conflict that has arisen from the existing institutional situation (rules in place): the responsibility currently falls on the owners to ascertain waiters make at least minimum wage, waiters are guaranteed no more than minimum and patrons have no responsibility outside of potential social obligations that encourage tipping. In the process of exploring these rules, the stakeholders should become clear. This accounting of the situation makes it more obvious that there is interdependence between restaurant owners, waiters and those that tip (or do not). The LEP model also gives the analyst room to envision several different structures for addressing interdependence and consider their performance (how they impact the involved parties), and whether they yield different results. In this case, we would ask who is paying what costs (consider increased prices, labor bill, take-home pay, etc.) to whom, or increased cost burden by party. It would also be reasonable to estimate other performance impacts on the involved parties, such as lost or increased revenue, patron and waiter happiness, etc.

These options are of course not the only ones that might be considered. An increase in the minimum wage would also be an alternative for which impact analysis could be conducted. In that case, the makeup of rights and duties would look largely the same, but we would expect some obvious performance changes. An empirical analysis of this type could be carried out comparing states across time in the U.S. who have different policies. This type of research could occur using both a case study based approach or a more quantitative approach with econometric or statistical analysis depending on data availability and the type of research question that the analyst wishes to answer.

THINK ABOUT IT ...
Performance Feedback and Institutional Change

Other characteristics of the physical world, such as habits, influence interdependence. Remember our discussion of formal and informal institutions from Chapter 1. Informal institutions, while not codified in some legal document or statute, can be just as prevalent, if not more so, than formal rules. In a conflict involving the minimum wage for tipped workers, it would be important to consider the cultural tipping dynamics that are present (or not) in the process of outlining the entire situation. If the minimum wage for tipped workers were eliminated, for instance, how might tipping norms change over time? Would the change be different if this were done on a state level? National level? What if tipped workers were suddenly paid a living wage? Changes in structure can trigger institutional change over time in the institutional situation.

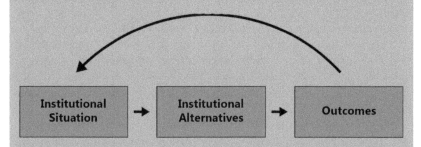

Figure 4.2   Institutional feedback

While we focus in this text on short-run impact analysis that holds the institutional situation constant, it is important to remember that the changes we make are part of a larger feedback loop that is always changing (Figure 4.2). These changes over time become the new institutional situation with its own interdependencies and so on. Just as people are constantly changing, so too are the institutions and situations we create and partake in. This may seem overwhelming, but it is the reality of the social sciences.

In summary: whenever an institutional detail influences the construction or potential performance of a conflict, it is important to take note and consider potential institutional feedback, or changes in behavior that may occur as a result and impact performance over time.

4.5   PUTTING IT ALL TOGETHER

The first step of the LEP framework involves laying out the situation, or everything that is going on. Like most first steps of theoretical models, it involves observation. Imagine that when you begin an analysis, you are first an investigator, and later an analyst or economist (or whatever your title may be). Before moving any further forward, like a detective, you must get your bearings and figure out what is really going on. Gathering as much information as possible about the context in which a problem occurs is key to understanding potential alternatives and outcomes.

An important underlying theme across all of these examples is the nature of comparison and what an analyst can say in comparing institutional alternatives as described in Hohfeldian language. As said best by Schmid (2006):

> The institutional resolution of the interdependence requires a moral judgment of whose interests count. No feature of a good or a situation dictates the appropriate institution. Every interdependence creates an externality and the policy issue is who creates externalities for whom. Where interdependent interests exist, choice of whose interests are to count is a power issue. To have a right is to be able to coerce others to do without or to meet the owner's terms. Where there is interdependence there is a formal or informal right to direct the interdependence and thus affect performance. However clear the right appears, it creates *de facto* opportunities. Each institutional alternative must be compared in terms of economic performance. However, unless the analyst can specify a normatively determined criteria for choosing between alternatives, they should be very cautious in making statements about which alternative is preferred.

Using impact analysis, the root of the conflict (interdependence) can not only be clarified, but different methods (institutional structures) of addressing the conflict may be compared. As you work through the following sections, ask yourself these questions:

1.   What is the institutional structure present?
    a.   Rules for making rules?
    b.   Rules in use?

2. What does this existing structure tell us about the interdependence present?

    a. By carefully specifying the key relationships amongst agents in a situation (in Hohfeldian terms) the analyst can begin to understand the incentives towards action that exist and may or may not be exercised.

3. What would a change in these rules (or the implementation of a rule, if there is none) mean for those involved?

    a. What assumptions are you making about behavior?

        i. How might it change?

Foundation topics in institutions from Chapter 1 and the language of Hohfeldian jural relations introduced in Chapter 2 can be used to help answer each of these. From there, we consider measures of conduct and performance, rounding out our model of institutional impact analysis. Refer to Figure 4.3 for an easy visual reminder of steps in the LEP framework.

4.6 CHAPTER RECAP

- The **LEP model for institutional analysis** serves as a tool for understanding how alternative institutional structures address instances of human interdependence and subsequent substantive economic outcomes of wealth and its distribution through the addition of a taxonomy of jural relations to describe and compare institutional structures.
- The **institutional situation** is about understanding the nature of interdependence between parties or actors in the economy. It is made up of the **interdependence** or interdependencies in question and the current **institutional structure**.
- Hohfeldian language and terms are used to describe the nature of the interdependence and institutions involved in a given situation.
- The **structure** is the independent variable of the analysis. These are the institutional alternatives that are available, holding the institutional situation, including the current rules for making rules or other higher-level institutions, constant.
- Empirical analysis will often be based on comparisons of institutional alternatives across time or geography. Both qualitative and quantitative approaches should be considered.
- **Economic performance** in the comparison of institutional alternatives should include distributional consequences across stakeholders.
- Analysts should be cautious of making statements about preferred alternatives without a normatively determined set of criteria.

Situation & Interdependence
Describe situation.
- Investigate. Gather as much potentially useful information as efficiently as possible to have on hand as you work through the more formal part of the analysis. **Be specific.**
  - Things to include: Parties involved, goods involved, characteristics, possible laws involved, etc.
- Form problem statements/questions.
- Form more specific questions/testable hypotheses.

Structure
Conduct Hohfeldian Legal Analysis.
- Lay out the current rules-in-use/jural relations identified during investigation of the Situation.
- Lay out rules-in-use for potential alternatives.

Performance
Conduct Hohfeldian Legal Analysis.
- Identify outcomes for each involved party.
- Be clear when a party is not included.
- Be clear also about behavioral assumptions (and any other such assumptions).
- Should coincide directly with Hohfeldian analysis.
- Things to include: estimated costs/benefits in terms of money, time, life, or some other metric used by the analyst. Be clear about metric used and understand potential issues (such as power, who gets what, etc.)

Figure 4.3   The Legal-Economic Performance framework cheat sheet

NOTES

1. From the 1970s up until his retirement in 2006, A. Allan Schmid worked to develop and refine the SSP model of institutional analysis. The model was developed and expanded through the books *Property, power and public choice* and then through the later book, *Conflict and cooperation* (Schmid, 1987, 2004). The SSP model includes the first S – understanding the characteristics of the good under

consideration and the nature of interdependence; the second S – the rules of the game that determine who has rights versus duties in light of the interdependence defined in step 1; and the final P – which outlines the distributional outcome of the rules as currently expressed. Schmid distinguishes between long-run institutional change theories, heavily focused on the first S of the model, and institutional impact theories, focused on alternatives considered in the structure part of the model.

2. Given the static nature of our analysis, we focus only on changes in formal institutions as alternatives. While informal institutions can certainly change or be changed over time, such analysis falls under institutional change analysis (for which Hohfeld has not been applied).

3. As a clue, the word "externality" indicates interdependence. See Schmid (1972, 2004).

4. Constitutions are another obvious example. The Constitution of the U.S. provides the foundation for the way laws can be made downstream – this plays a part in understanding not just the way the current rules were formed, but also the way future rules may be structured. It can be important and helpful to know the current structure and how it was formed in order to identify key issues of interdependence.

5. Examples of each of these are given in Schmid (2004, pp. 139–162), as applied specifically to the SSP model, similar to our model here except for the lack of more formal legal analysis as applied to interdependence.

PART II

Applications

In the following case chapters, we provide simplified examples of legal cases or conflicts found in the real world. We work through each of these unique situations using various aspects of the LEP framework in part or whole. The micro-institutional situations considered include a labor dispute at a popular ride-sharing enterprise (both in the U.S. and United Kingdom (U.K.)), issues of public accommodation and discrimination in the U.S., some structural considerations and performance issues in the common-pool resources of fisheries, and the interdependencies involved in a union organization issue in the U.S.

While the cases given here can certainly be built upon in class as coursework, the options of alternatives or supplemental assignments are endless. To assist with these cases here and any potential future cases used, we provide an appendix of basic legal terminology (Appendix G), as well as case briefs when applicable (Appendices A–F). This is intended to give non-legal scholars the basic information they need to consider the case situations and others they may encounter. Each case includes issues for further thought, and in no means provides a comprehensive analysis of all aspects of the conflicts presented. We hope they are useful for discussion as well as practice in applying the tools introduced in Chapters 1–4.

5. Uber versus drivers

5.1 SITUATION

As ride sharing becomes a more ubiquitous form of transport and a major source of income for many drivers, labor disputes between ride-sharing drivers and the company (owner of the app) that they work through are increasingly common. In recent years, cases have appeared before both U.S. and U.K. courts regarding worker classification and, more specifically, their labor rights. These workers are seeking better means of negotiating for various rights and benefits within their respective workplaces.

In several cases, Uber has identified drivers as independent contractors who therefore lack many of the rights afforded to non-gig workers under U.K. and U.S. law. This means reduced bargaining power for drivers as a group. Uber drivers take issue with this classification, claiming they fulfill the role of a regular employee as codified in various labor laws. The conflict has been developing in different ways in multiple places, all of which may be relevant for a general application of the LEP model.

5.1.1 Legal Background

London-area drivers for Uber London Ltd. and Uber Britannia Ltd. (parent company Uber BV) brought claims before the employment tribunal (ET) in the U.K. under the Employment Rights Act 1996, the National Minimum Wage Act 1998, and the Working Time Regulations 1998 and associated regulations for failure to pay the minimum wage and to provide paid leave (*Uber BV* v. *Aslam*, 2019). Uber denied that the claimants were at any time classified as "workers" under the acts, arguing instead that their drivers were self-employed independent contractors and therefore not entitled to the protection of those legislations. The ET found that the English laws did apply and that the claimants were "employed" and engaged in working time from the moment they switched the app on and were in their designated working area and able to accept assignments (*Uber BV*, 2019). Uber resisted, and in February 2021 the U.K.'s Supreme Court unanimously dismissed Uber's appeal, ruling that its drivers are workers, not independent contractors, with all the legal protections that entails (*Uber BV* v. *Aslam*, 2021). This judgment rested on five aspects of the findings made by the ET:

1. When a ride is booked, Uber sets the fare and drivers do not get to modify this rate or that which they are paid.
2. Uber imposed all contract terms on drivers with no say from drivers.
3. Once a driver has logged on to the app, they are still somewhat constrained to the number of rides they may decline without penalty.
4. Uber exercises significant control over all aspects of service provision, including the driver rating system that directly figures into continued employment with Uber.
5. Uber restricts the scope of the communication the driver may have with the passenger.

When all five aspects are considered, the court supported the initial judgment by the ET. As stated:

> Drivers are in a position of subordination and dependency in relation to Uber such that they have little or no ability to improve their economic position through professional or entrepreneurial skill. In practice the only way in which they can increase their earnings is by working longer hours while constantly meeting Uber's measures of performance ... The drivers were rightly found to be workers. (*Uber BV*, 2021)

As such, Uber must pay its drivers the national living wage and provide 28 days (about four weeks) paid holiday from the start of working time.

A similar case played out in the U.S. in the state of California. In *O'Connor* v. *Uber Techs* (2015) the U.S. District Court held that the drivers were presumptive employees of Uber, not independent contractors, because the drivers performed a service for Uber and Uber depended on its drivers' performance of services for its revenues (*O'Connor*, 2015). Given this decision, the burden now shifts to Uber to disprove an employment relationship. The Court further found that Uber was not entitled to summary judgment. They could only be granted one if "all facts and evidentiary inferences material to the employee/independent contractor determination are undisputed, and a reasonable jury viewing those undisputed facts and inferences could reach but one conclusion – that Uber's drivers are independent contractors as a matter of law" (*O'Connor*, 2015). Much of the decision hinged on "employment" tests laid out in a previous case (the Borello test), specifically how much control over work details the hirer retains the right to exercise. When evaluating the extent of control, the Supreme Court has emphasized that an employer's "right to discharge at will, without cause [is] strong evidence in support of an employment relationship" (*O'Connor*, 2015). The Court also utilized a number of secondary indicia of relevance to the employee/independent contractor determination including various work details such as type of occupation, degree of supervision and specialization, length of time services are provided, method of payment, etc.

In another case, the California Supreme Court reinterpreted and ultimately rejected the Borello test for determining whether workers should be classified as employees or independent contractors (*Dynamex Operations West, Inc.* v. *Superior Court*, 2018). The Court further embraced the standard that all workers are *presumed* to be employees, placing the burden on the hirer to prove otherwise using a newly adopted "ABC test." To successfully show that a worker is an independent contractor, the employer must provide documentation showing that three things are true:

1. the worker is free from control and direction in the performance of services;
2. the worker is performing work outside the usual course of the business of the hiring company; and
3. the worker is customarily engaged in an independently established trade, occupation or business (McNicholas and Poydock, 2019).

Building on this momentum, in September 2019, the California legislature passed Assembly Bill 5, requiring companies that hire independent contractors to reclassify them as employees, with few exceptions (AB5, 2019). The Bill went into effect in January 2020.

Legal challenges to AB5 and related efforts continue. In November 2020, 58 percent of California voters voted in favor of Proposition 22, which allows drivers for apps such as Uber to be classified as independent contractors instead of employees. This proposition undermined a large portion of AB5, including removing protections like access to workers' compensation, paid family leave and unemployment insurance that were included in the AB5 classification (Mollaneda, 2021). Such rulings also impact whether drivers are able to collectively bargain or unionize as a means of negotiating wages and other benefits. When the U.S. National Labor Relations Board ruled that Uber drivers are independent contractors and not employees, many groups acknowledged that they would have to focus on changing the rules at the municipal or state level (Romo, 2019) rather than targeting national support under the current administration.

5.2   INSTITUTIONAL ALTERNATIVES AND PERFORMANCE

In our LEP analysis, we consider a labor dispute between the ride-sharing company Uber and the drivers they employ. Given that this disagreement is taking place in the U.S., we focus on understanding current U.S. law in action.

The existing legal clashes and laws pertaining to workers in this space are all relevant background research. Further examination of contract agreements between the two parties make it clear that the conflict centers around murky definitions of the employment category in which the drivers belong. If drivers are independent contractors, then by current law they are not entitled to many of the benefits reserved for employees, but also must meet certain criteria that could modify the way Uber interacts with them.

Currently, conflict in the U.S. between drivers and ride-sharing companies such as Uber has revolved around not only whether drivers are independent contractors or not, but also what it means to be a contractor in this space. By Uber's accounts in the cases mentioned above, their drivers have little to no control or negotiating power over wages or other aspects of the job and are not able to unionize, while also enjoying none of the benefits like leave time and unemployment. Various courts and regulators have had the difficult task of attempting to define both categorizations while deciding which category drivers belong in. If a key characteristic of independent work is the ability to negotiate one's own wages and work conditions, for instance, this would impact the way Uber currently interacts with drivers. Similarly, if contractors are able to unionize, this would again modify the way Uber must interact with its current and potential drivers. If it is decided that contractors are a class of workers that cannot negotiate, cannot unionize, are subject to whatever rules the firm sets before them, can be fired at will, but hold the power to accept or reject these terms (also at will), Uber can continue to do what they want in this space (though given existing rules and laws, this classification will continue to face legal challenges).

We use Hohfeldian legal analysis and the general LEP framework to consider how this issue might play out (Table 5.1). Assuming for this analysis that the status quo is that contractors are subject to Uber's current employment practices and are unable to unionize, we consider alternative scenarios in which (1) drivers are classified as contractors (essentially the current state of things in many U.S. locales); (2) drivers are classified as employees and can unionize; and (3) classification of works is left up to the discretion of the company. For this third alternative we consider performance variations if the workers are able to bargain versus if they are not.

Uber and Uber drivers are interdependent because they each need the other to operate. The details of how they operate together, however, are a matter of contention. Under the first alternative, drivers are ruled to be independent contractors and are unable to unionize. This means they have exposure to Uber's employment choices regarding wages, benefits, etc., and Uber has the privilege to set these. Both have the power to end the relationship and the associated liability under conditions set by Californian law (mostly at will). If drivers are employees and *can* unionize, however, they have the right to

Table 5.1   *LEP framework: Uber versus drivers*

Problem/situation	Interdependence (parties/current structure)	Structure	Performance questions
CA Uber driver classification Drivers currently presumed contractors. Some demand to be classified as employees and entitled to those benefits and the ability to unionize. Legal precedent varies in this gig economy space. The issue has been approached from multiple directions in many different places	Interdependence between Uber and drivers over how drivers are classified and whether or not they have the power to unionize	1. Drivers are contractors, cannot unionize 2. Drivers are employees, can unionize 3. Up to the company's discretion	1. Lower costs for Uber; higher for drivers (others?); no bargaining means higher transaction costs for workers, less representation 2. Workers entitled to minimum wage, employee benefits, etc. Cost of reclassifying might pass costs on to consumers 3. If drivers have bargaining power: results likely closer to (2); if drivers are not allowed to bargain: results likely closer to (1)

minimum wage and other benefits workers are entitled to, in addition to the legal right to unionize. Uber has the corresponding duty to provide these benefits and to not interfere with unionization efforts to a point. In the third scenario, worker classification is left to the discretion of Uber, who can choose to label their drivers either way. This gives a Hohfeldian power to make this choice to Uber and imposes a Hohfeldian liability on drivers. In this scenario we consider what the performance outcomes might look like if things are left to Uber's discretion when the workers have the privilege to unionize versus when they do not.

A ruling broadly favoring the classification of these kinds of workers as contractors has considerable performance implications for workers, businesses and the general public. If a worker is considered an independent contractor, the employer does not bear responsibility for paying towards social security, payroll taxes, unemployment, state employment, workers' compensation insurance, among all the other state and other statutes pertaining to hours, time off and wages (including providing a minimum wage). These costs fall on other parties, such as the worker, when they are classified as independent contractors. Not being able to unionize introduces high bargaining costs (transaction costs) that would make it virtually impossible for drivers to negotiate wages or other such benefits.

If the worker is classified as an employee *and* can bargain, costs will rise for Uber as they now cover the expense of many of the benefits mentioned above. Through the course of bargaining, it will be possible to achieve more with reduced transaction costs. Drivers will have greater representation in general. Depending on the rules for classification as an employee, some flexibility in employment could be lost. It is possible that fares may also increase as Uber passes higher costs on to consumers. These would be good potential outcomes to further explore both qualitatively and quantitatively.

Under our third scenario, we have the classic "let the market decide" response. Yet again, this rule would be predicated on what other existing rules and laws are at work in the space. Uber is essentially allowed to decide what classifies as an independent contractor, avoiding the costs associated with various rules and programs for employees while setting the majority of the terms for employment, limited only by rules that apply to all individuals regardless of classification. If they are able to set the rules, workers are able to bargain, and we assume profit-maximizing behavior on behalf of the firm, performance will likely be relatively close to scenario 2. Uber will retain the privilege to set wages, etc., and drivers will be largely exposed to these choices. Through bargaining, however, drivers will be represented and able to negotiate in some capacity with Uber. Without this ability to unionize and bargain, performance will likely be very similar to the first scenario.

Under all three scenarios, drivers will not be impacted equally. Some drivers, as seen during the lead up to Proposition 22, supported remaining labeled as independent contractors for various personal, political and financial reasons. These preferences would also be useful to explore in a more fleshed-out impact analysis.

5.3   FURTHER NOTES

In the LEP analysis above we consider several alternatives that hinge on a very specific definition of the characteristics of what it means to be an independent contractor. If these are different or change in the real world (note: they are), the Hohfeldian relations and performance piece will change. For instance, if a key trait of independent contract work is the ability to maintain a network of relationships with individual clients such as the riders in the vehicle, this would greatly impact Uber's current way of doing business. It is possible that the definition of a contractor is decided to be such that Uber decide that they are better off classifying their drivers as regular employees, with all the benefits and protections that entails. Furthermore, there could be any number of modifications or interpretations of new or existing labor laws and regulations that could modify work in the ride-sharing space and gig economy in general. The possibilities outlined here can easily be modified and expanded.

6. *Masterpiece Cakeshop, Ltd. v. Colorado Civil Rights Commission*

6.1   SITUATION

As discussed in Chapter 2, anti-discrimination or public accommodation laws are a topic of much debate. These laws prohibit the discrimination by a "public accommodation" enterprise against individual consumers based on several potential characteristics such as race, gender, marital status and religion. A "public accommodation" is a commercial enterprise that is open to non-employees. There have been several notable cases in this realm, including the Supreme Court case *Masterpiece Cakeshop, Ltd.* v. *Colorado Civil Rights Commission* (2018).

The so-called "gay cake" case was an important legal and social event in 2016 that helped set the stage for the issue of competing Hohfeldian rights and duties. It was taken up by the U.S. Supreme Court and was argued in 2017 and decided in 2018. See Appendix B for a brief of the Supreme Court case.

The Masterpiece Cakeshop was owned by proprietor Jack C. Phillips. In 2012, the soon-to-be-wedded Charlie Craig and his mother entered the establishment seeking a wedding cake. Their request was refused. Phillips proceeded to explain he would not make a wedding cake as it would imply that he endorsed or accepted a same-sex marriage. This, he stated, was against his religious beliefs. Craig and his partner proceeded to file a charge with the Colorado Civil Rights Commission of discrimination in contravention of Colorado law.

In response to this charge, the cakeshop did not deny that it discriminated, but that its proprietor's rights of religious freedom were more important than the anti-discrimination rights of the same-sex couple as laid out in the Colorado Anti-Discrimination Act (CADC). The couple took their complaint to the Colorado Civil Rights Commission who took up the case, ultimately ruling that the cakeshop was in violation of the act. Phillips then sued the Commission in federal court. The case eventually ended up at the U.S. Supreme Court.

6.1.1   Legal Background

The defendants in this case presented their argument to the court, citing public accommodation and anti-discrimination laws that have a long history in the U.S. They argued that the state of Colorado was not forcing or compelling Phillips to speak but rather that he could not discriminate against a gay couple for a product that he would willingly provide to other customers. The plaintiffs argued that to allow this business to not serve certain customers because of religious concerns would (1) open the doors to many public businesses denying customers for similar attributes and (2) be an unprecedented reinterpretation of law (*Masterpiece Cakeshop*, 2018).

One brief of note filed in support of the Commission and the same-sex couple was from a group of over 200 bakers and chefs including celebrities like Anthony Bourdain and Jose Andres. They argued that while cooking and baking can be creative endeavors, the final product is to be eaten and not protected under the first amendment (Shah and Cicconi, 2017). Further, they argued that chefs and bakers do not lose creative control in their choices – only that they must prepare for anyone who enters their shop or establishment what they offer to someone else.

In direct contradiction, Phillips and his lawyers argued that the state is in fact attempting to force Phillips to speak and in doing so is infringing on his free exercise and freedom of speech. In the brief for Mr. Phillips, the lawyers write, "Yet they do not deny that Colorado permits secular cake artists to decline orders that express 'offensive messages' critical of same-sex marriage" (*Masterpiece Cakeshop*, 2018). The argument relies heavily on the fact that Phillips is an artist and involved in a creative endeavor and that in this case he cannot be compelled to speak in a way contrary to his religious beliefs through his art.

In support of Phillips' case, several groups and scholars submitted their own briefs. A group calling themselves "law and economics scholars" submitted an amicus curia in *Masterpiece Cakeshop* (2018) supporting the claims of religious expression over the claims of anti-discrimination laws. In their brief, they discuss the fact that, "accordingly, in the absence of monopoly, there is no economic basis to rule out the granting of exceptions from state anti-discrimination laws to those limited by religious convictions. Refusing to do so reduces social welfare" (*Masterpiece Cakeshop*, 2018). They further claim that "Conversely, allowing the state to coerce religiously motivated merchants into compliance with its antidiscrimination law would diminish social welfare, reduce freedom, and harm an unwilling market participant coerced into compliance along with everyone else who respects and supports his or her views." These arguments hinge on an assumed outcome reliant on social welfare and presumably the Pareto efficiency criterion. Per this argument, coercion is one sided and would occur if the state forces its views on the merchant. It is however not coercion if the government places the rights on the side of the merchant. This decision is labeled "freedom" and in turn is seen as welfare enhancing (as opposed to welfare-reducing effects of a decision in the opposite direction).

Following these arguments, the Supreme Court decided in Phillips' favor. Justice Kennedy wrote the majority opinion, noting the hostility and unevenness shown by the Commission toward Phillips' religious views. The majority wrote:

> Given the State's position at the time, there is some force to Phillips' argument that he was not unreasonable in deeming his decision lawful. State law at the time also afforded storekeepers some latitude to decline to create specific messages they considered offensive. Indeed, while the instant enforcement proceedings were pending, the State Civil Rights Division concluded in at least three cases that a baker acted lawfully in declining to create cakes with decorations that demeaned gay persons or gay marriages. Phillips too was entitled to a neutral and respectful consideration of his claims in all the circumstances of the case. (*Masterpiece Cakeshop*, 2018)

While the majority opinion was written by Justice Kennedy, Justice Thomas and Gorsuch agreed but also wrote their own concurring opinions. Most notably, Justice Thomas argued that, while in general the majority opinion was correct, it did not go far enough and that in fact Phillips' work was an act of free speech and not just the act of making a cake. In this case, these concurring and dissenting opinions create a broader context of Hohfeldian issues to consider. Thomas' concurrence, if it had the force of law, would place more Hohfeldian power with the defendant (Phillips and his religious objections), to invoke producer sovereignty and reject a customer as opposed to the customer's Hohfeldian right as expressed in the Colorado public accommodation law.

The degree of uncertainty over the interpretation of the majorities' findings certainly will have an impact on economic decision making in the realms of consumption and production. That uncertainty is evident in a variety of competing interpretations by commentators and legal scholars over the ruling. This means that future conflicts between consumers and producers will occur within the context of uncertainty over the exact nature of the institutional regime. The views and interpretations of lower-court judges in regards to the Supreme Court ruling will therefore be critical.

6.1.2 Economic Theory and Research Notes on Anti-Discrimination Laws

A group calling themselves "behavioral science and economics scholars" filed one brief of particular importance to the economics debate. One of the main arguments these scholars made is that there are major flaws in the neoclassical models being used by the other side to claim that discrimination will be eliminated by the free market (Hofmann and Mason, 2017). These scholars claimed that discrimination based on sexual orientation, while less studied, is likely to follow the same path as racial discrimination if current policy prescriptions continue. They tied their arguments to empirical evidence that strongly suggests that many decades after the end of Jim Crow laws in the southern U.S. there remains a great deal of discrimination.

The economics discipline has perspectives on anti-discrimination laws and public accommodation laws in both a theoretical and empirical context. One important idea from economics is the concept of consumer sovereignty. This is the idea that the individual consumer's preference dictates the output of the economy versus for example state or collective preferences. Consumer sovereignty is recognized as being created by economist William Howard Hutt in 1936 (Persky, 1993). The idea was not justified on economic outcomes at that time but as an analogy to freedom in the context of political voting in a democracy. It is a means versus an ends argument. The other clear point Hutt made was that producers would have to follow consumers and would take second place in the economy (Persky, 1993).

This consumer sovereignty idea does not address the issue of producer rights or preferences. What happens when a producer refuses to serve a consumer? Is there an economic theory to address this concern? Economics Nobel Laureate Gary Becker, working on his dissertation in 1955, directly addressed the economics of discrimination. Becker's argument, in simplified form, was that discrimination hurt both the discriminator and the discriminated party. More importantly, he wrote that over time this economic discrimination would falter and fall away as competitive forces went to work and drove the discriminating establishments out of business. At bottom, these arguments rely on the mechanism of competition to drive out discriminators. By this logic, no discriminating producer should ever exist for any length of time as it should eventually be driven out of business. Here we can see the connection to consumer sovereignty and that consumption preferences will ultimately drive markets.

Not surprisingly, economic research in the area of anti-discrimination or public accommodation laws focuses on the outcomes versus means or processes. For example, researchers have taken advantage of differences in state-level anti-discrimination laws in housing and labor markets to assess institutional alternatives. Collins (2001), using state-level fair employment laws in the 1940s and 1950s prior to the federal Civil Rights Act of 1964, found that these did improve the relative labor market outcomes for African Americans. In particular, he found that the laws passed in the 1940s were more effective than those passed in the 1950s and that African American women fared better than African American men.

John Yinger (1998) examined the general question of whether prejudiced firms were being driven out of business by unprejudiced firms. He finds evidence that consumer discrimination remains strongly intact across many makers including automobiles, housing and credit access. If the failure of prejudiced firms is going to happen, it may be over decades rather than years or shorter time periods.

6.1.3   Hohfeldian Analysis

The case presented here features a bifurcation in the social choice between Hohfeldian rights and duties and the potential implications of alternative institutional regimes. It is important to note that the judicial rulings present different institutional regimes in this case and others.

Moving beyond the complexity of the legal arguments, the basic issue is one involving the choice of markets and who has what rights. A ruling for the defendant Phillips would mean potentially that, in general terms, business endeavors that are considered creative or artistic cannot be compelled to speak through their products by public regulation like public accommodation laws. This scenario would give power to Phillips to say no to a customer based on their views or actions. A ruling for the plaintiff would mean some creative business endeavors would potentially be required under law to provide a product or service to all protected consumer classes regardless of objections. The plaintiff in this case, a same-sex couple, would have power because they can enter a public accommodation business and expect service. Of course, Supreme Court rulings are rarely ever this simple.

At the core of the case is a conflict over competing rights. These competing rights and duties can be simplified for the purposes of analysis. On the one hand, the CADC has a provision that certain groups, in this case based on disability, creed, sexual orientation, sex, color and other characteristics, have the right to be provided service in places of public accommodation. The Colorado Civil Rights Commission as the adjudicating body had authority to implement the law. The same-sex couple claimed that they have a right to be served in a place of public accommodation (the cakeshop). This was a Hohfeldian right, in rem, that they held per the statute, and placed a duty on any public accommodation establishment located in the state of Colorado. This represents one potential institutional regime that has an impact on economic performance and distribution.

On the other side, the cakeshop claimed that it had a right under the first amendment of the U.S. Constitution regarding free speech and religious freedom. In essence, the cakeshop claimed a Hohfeldian right to decide who to serve and that religious views could serve as a factor in deciding who to make a cake for. The duty would then be placed on those who came into the establishment to refrain from having a cake or other product from this cakeshop.

The comparative institutional impact question centers around this question of who has rights, or whose rights "count." Where do the rights of religious freedom lie vis-à-vis the anti-discrimination laws? What rights, specifically, do these entail? At its heart, this question cannot be answered using the efficiency criterion. Both alternatives are economically efficient. The economist can ask what the performance implications of the various alternatives are both in the short and long term.

6.2   INSTITUTIONAL ALTERNATIVES AND ECONOMIC PERFORMANCE

Based on this background material, this section reviews some broad institutional alternatives that may exist in this situation. We can consider several institutional structures for analysis.

The first institutional alternative would be a legal regime where the potential groups of consumers as defined in law have rights to be provided a good or service by a public accommodation establishment in that particular jurisdiction. In this case, the public accommodation establishments have a Hohfeldian duty to provide those particular goods or services that they generally sell to the public within certain limits.[1]

Several possible performance implications follow from this initial legal or institutional regime. Those public accommodation establishments whose owners or proprietors have certain principled objections to certain characteristics or activities may attempt to evade public accommodation classification or perhaps move jurisdictions (or simply go out of business). This is explored by Milton Friedman and others who write that discriminating businesses would likely fail the competitive test over time (Friedman, 1962, 1970). This could lead to shifts in the allocation of investments in the sector overall and in the distribution of those investment decisions across different types of owners. For instance, in an amicus curiae brief submitted in *Masterpiece Cakeshop* (2018) by the Denver Regional Chamber of Commerce it was argued that anti-discrimination laws were in fact pro-business and had helped develop the strength of the Denver region's economic markets (Schoenfeld et al., 2017). The Chamber of Commerce cited evidence from a study by the Michigan Civil Rights Commission that found that a lack of anti-discrimination institutions would be harmful to economic development and talent attraction in a region.

The second institutional alternative is one where the public accommodation business can decide which consumers it will serve (allowing principled objections to certain characteristics or businesses). The public accommodation business has a Hohfeldian right to exclude certain consumers and those consumers are under a duty not to respond.

There are several economic performance considerations under this structure. One possibility is that the groups of consumers who lose access to the market or certain establishments may create their own businesses, leading to shifts in investment and consumption patterns. A pattern of market segregation may occur with different levels of business availability and pricing. This market segregation may mean certain consumer classes may pay more than others, for instance, which may have economic welfare implications. Another potential implication is that various groups will tend to isolate themselves socially and economically, as there is greater and greater fragmentation and differentiation in the marketplace.

An empirical analysis of this situation would of course require some measures of variables. There are several different approaches one could take. One approach would be to examine how lower courts interpret and rule on these types of cases over time to determine if a specific pattern exists. Another approach would be to assess the impact on whether market segregation occurs and to what extent in states that do or do not have a law similar to Colorado's. Public accommodation laws are generally state level, although some cities may have their own specific versions of these laws as well, and all of these cases provide variation to allow for investigation.

Both institutional alternatives will lead to some shift in investment, consumption and production patterns. It is possible that this ruling will not change the overall production or consumption of wedding cakes or other bakery products. For some of the participants in this debate, the point is not about economic outcomes per se, but about the perception that the existence of a baker who is able to act in a prejudicial manner is inappropriate. For others, the issue is about the new concept of producer sovereignty which is not typically found in economic textbooks. In textbooks, producers are generally viewed as profit-maximizing entities who operate with a certain technology and respond to consumer preferences. Each of those resulting decision patterns are economically efficient and Pareto non-comparable.

6.3   FURTHER NOTES

This case has garnered a significant amount of attention in the press and an ongoing series of academic articles. It will likely have an impact over a very long period of time in the context of the battle over rights in the U.S. system. The example is presented in summary form and not with attention to all of the legal issues, details and questions raised.

At one level the basic legal question, which has important economic implications, is whether religious expression rights supersede rights regarding the ability to purchase a commercial product in a public accommodation business. Legal scholars have noted that the court did not find for the plaintiff strictly on the grounds of free speech. They also found that the record showed the Civil Rights Commission exhibiting hostility towards Phillips and his religious beliefs (Nejaime and Siegel, 2018). That said, legal scholars argue over the scope and importance of the case over time. Some will argue that the case is part of a long line of litigation seeking to expand free speech to commercial and business activities. Others may argue that its implications are limited.

For example, Nejaime and Siegle (2018) argue that in fact the *Masterpiece Cakeshop* (2018) ruling shows that the court is not creating new exemptions for religious expression in public accommodation laws but rather religion must be treated neutrally with regards to the law. While legal scholars undoubtedly differ on some of the details and nuances regarding the case, there does appear to be a growing consensus that the court was ruling in regard to the fact that Phillips did not receive equal treatment as compared to the secular counterparts who also wished not to provide a product to a consumer. This is an obvious critical difference that has important implications for consumers.

NOTE

1.   These limits mean that those rights are not absolute and will end if for example the consumer cannot provide adequate payment or potentially other conditions. The Hohfeldian right in this case ends and the duty switches to an exposure if the consumer is unable to pay or meet other financial terms.

7. Cedar Point Nursery v. Hassid (CA Agricultural Labor Relations Board)

7.1 SITUATION

In 1975, the state of California's Agricultural Labor Relations Board passed a regulation that allowed farm union organizers to access their agricultural employer's property in a temporary fashion in specified non-work areas to communicate with current and potential union members (CA Agricultural Labor Relations Board, 2021). This was called the access regulation. This regulation has been in place for many decades and allows a union organization to access private property to contact and potentially gain new union members. The basic argument for the access regulation was that potential union members had very irregular schedules and the ability to communicate with them was much more effective if it occurred during work hours at the employer's premises.

In 2015, the agricultural employer Cedar Point Nursery, a strawberry grower, claimed that union organizers from the United Farm Workers Association accessed employer property without proper notice (Howe, 2021b). This led to a filing in 2016 by the agricultural employer against the California Agricultural Labor Board and the access regulation (and in essence against the rights of the employee unions). The employer (Cedar Point Nursery) argued that the access regulation represented a "per se" or "physical" property taking and was unconstitutional. Victoria Hassid served as the commissioner of the California Agricultural Labor Relations Board and is the named defendant in the case of *Cedar Point Nursery* v. *Hassid*.

7.1.1 Legal Basics

The case revolves around a key Hohfeldian relation: the Hohfeldian right of the labor unions to access employer property under certain conditions and the corresponding Hohfeldian duty of agricultural employers to not interfere with this access under the rule. The status quo institutional regime in California is one that was created by the California Agricultural Labor Board in the 1970s. The regulation states that agricultural labor unions can access on a limited basis private property to communicate with current and potential union members (CA Agricultural Labor Relations Board, 2021). The justification for this rule is that it is often very difficult to communicate with laborers off work hours. This status quo rule creates a right for agricultural labor unions, under certain conditions, to enter someone else's property and communicate with these employees. The law also creates the duty that agricultural employers may not interfere with these union activities. The right ends if the activity is attempted outside of certain fairly restrictive conditions and the law of private trespass with the employer's right to exclude from their property is then reasserted.

Under this status quo legal regime, the agricultural labor unions clearly benefit from greater access to current and potential laborers which can expand and retain membership and improve their bargaining and financial strength and stability. The union's opportunity set is expanded by the status quo set of rules. On the other hand, the agricultural employer's opportunity set is restricted given this law. Neither side argued in the Supreme Court, it should be clarified, that the status quo rule in any meaningful way reduced the production or operations of the agricultural employer. If it did, the agricultural union organizers were under a duty to remove themselves from the property.

In this case, the agricultural employer was attempting to shift the distribution of the legal regime in their favor and expand their own opportunity while closing or withdrawing options from the union opportunity set. In other words, the agents are competing over the sphere of mutual coercion (see Chapter 3). The employers are arguing that this legal regime shift should occur because the government (in enforcing the rights of the union organizers) is engaging in a so-called "property taking." A taking is defined under the fifth amendment of the U.S. Constitution. The U.S. Constitution specifically states that "Nor shall private property be taken for public use, without just compensation" (Library of Congress, n.d.). In very basic terms it means that the government cannot deprive a citizen who owns property of that property without just compensation.

In a case like this, the analyst needs to understand the legal background to fully appreciate the institutional alternatives that may be examined in an impact analysis. This provision of the Constitution was reshaped following the American Civil War and the passage of the fourteenth amendment. This amendment stated that the state could not deprive citizens of life, liberty or property without due process. Due process, very simply, means that a person is accorded fair treatment through the recognized court or judicial system. The fifth and fourteenth amendments were read and interpreted together by the Supreme Court (Asbridge, forthcoming). In essence, this meant that if a government was exercising "police powers" or regulatory authority it did not have to compensate the person for that taking (as long as due process was followed), but if the government was exercising imminent domain, then it would have to compensate the person.

In an important case *Pennsylvania Coal Co.* v. *Mahon* (1922; hereafter *Mahon*) in the early twentieth century, Justice Oliver Wendell Holmes wrote the opinion that helped establish much of the legal principles around government takings for the twentieth century (Brauneis, 1996). The case was about the legal relationship between a homeowner and coal-mining company in Pennsylvania. The homeowners, when purchasing the property for their residence under the contract, agreed that coal mining could still take place in the vicinity. The homeowners had agreed that they had a Hohfeldian right with the specific case of coal mining in certain areas. The coal-mining company retained the right to mine in these areas although they had given up rights to the specific areas where the homeowners resided. Subsequent to these events, the state government then passed a law prohibiting coal mining in the vicinity of homeowners if it caused problems for the homes themselves. The law essentially removed the rights that the coal-mining company had secured under the contract, essentially giving the homeowners a right to a coal-mining-free vicinity and the coal-mining company a duty to not mine.

The essence of the case and Supreme Court ruling was about the status of the move from a right to an exposure for the coal-mining company. Justice Holmes, writing in the majority opinion, stated that this had been a per se taking and required compensation (Brauneis, 1996). The change in legal status by the government statute had severely restricted the coal company's economic options and reduced the value of the company in the court's majority opinion. Since the *Mahon* case, the Supreme Court has generally followed a basic set of principles in regard to takings law (Brauneis, 1996). Over the past century, the court has promulgated several different rules and principles that help dictate how lower courts will deal with cases. This system has led to a situation where those claiming a "taking" are often hard pressed to prove their case.

Since *Mahon*, the Supreme Court has added greatly to takings law and in turn defined new institutional structures that guide the economy. The court made the distinction between regulatory and physical or per se takings. A physical taking would require compensation and a regulatory taking would not (Asbridge, forthcoming). A physical taking would be based on the permanent and physical invasion of an owner's property. Later, U.S. courts began to recognize a distinction between a regulatory taking and a per se or physical taking. U.S. law recognized that governments could use police powers to regulate private economic agents for the general safety, health and welfare of the community or society (Asbridge, forthcoming). These regulations could potentially lead to a regulatory taking. In a simplified sense, a regulatory taking occurred when, "A regulatory taking is not an actual physical invasion, however, but a restriction to a certain degree on a landholder's right to use the land in a certain way" (Pack, 2002, p. 396).

Even within this general framework, there was a great deal of debate as to whether the change involved a new use or regulation of an existing use (Asbridge, forthcoming). Generally speaking, the Supreme Court has created rules that require weighing against one another the extent of the burden of the rule on the private agent and the strength of the public interest in undertaking the action (Asbridge, forthcoming). Of course, this weighing process also means some degree of uncertainty at times regarding whether a policy action is ultimately a takings or not. Again, as the rules evolve, different institutional structures are being created and reshaped in the economy.

A rule that limits or severely restricts eminent domain would create a very different world than one where government regulation is broadly conceived of as a taking. For the sake of analysis, it is useful to consider who the competing agents are even if the government is standing in as an enforcement agency. In the takings cases, there are often competing sides, putting aside the government as enforcer, who are acting. In *Cedar Point*, the California Agricultural Labor Board was being called on as a remedial power from the farmworkers' union organization to help enforce the rights that the union claimed it had under California law and was being prevented from exercising by the employer. A ruling in favor of the union could result in more union activity and perhaps greater wages and benefits for those workers. At the same time, a union-favorable ruling may lead to other consequences such as fewer jobs being offered or other restrictions from the employer.

7.1.2   *Cedar Point* Case Filings and Decision

The agricultural employer and their supporters argued that this was a clear taking of their property and in particular a removal of the stick from the bundle of rights that gives owners the right to exclude anyone from their property. The bundle of rights metaphor was invoked in several plaintiff-friendly briefs. The Cato Institute brief for example argued that "the strands in [Cedar Point Nursery's] bundle of rights – should be accorded the same protection from state interference as those of life and liberty" (Shapiro et al., 2020). The Southeastern Legal Foundation and Mountain States Legal Foundation also cite the importance of exclusion as part of the bundle of rights approach (Thomas et al., 2020; Wohlgemuth and McDonald, 2020). These groups were all arguing that California law took away a critical piece of the bundle of rights, the right to exclusion, and impacted the economic opportunity set of the plaintiff in this case.

The other side, arguing for the defendants in this case, were pursuing a different view of takings and property rights. A brief was filed by a group calling themselves legal historians who are identified as scholars from law schools. Their basic argument is that the right to exclude has never been an absolute right. All the way back to the beginning of the history of the country, the government has been given access to private property for a variety of reasons (Berger et al., 2021). Their ultimate argument is that there is no absolute right (or Hohfeldian duty) to property and that reasonable exceptions have always existed similar to California's laws.

Here we see the different sides arguing for their Hohfeldian view to be upheld. The economic importance of the Supreme Court decision cannot be underestimated given the number of parties arguing for both sides. These arguments present a rich array of alternatives that analysts can consider in impact analysis. The debate between the parties may be framed as government interference, as in the Cato Institute brief, or as a promotion of the ability of government to act. The LEP approach is to avoid such dichotomies. We should view the debate, regardless of the rhetoric of either side, as one of whose interests count, as opposed to government versus no government.

7.2 INSTITUTIONAL ALTERNATIVES AND ECONOMIC PERFORMANCE

What are the other alternatives that we can imagine in this situation? The first scenario to examine is the one based on the decision of the U.S. Supreme Court.

The court majority, with an opinion written by Chief Justice Roberts, ruled that indeed the union organizers had, via the state of California law, unconstitutionally infringed upon the employer's property rights. This decision will have important consequences for the direction between appropriation and regulation in takings law and foreshadow even further changes in the future.

The Roberts opinion squarely sides with the idea, building on the ideas of William Blackstone, that exclusion from property must be absolute and is the foundation of a democratic form of government. As the opinion states:

> We cannot agree that the right to exclude is an empty formality, subject to modification at the government's pleasure. On the contrary, it is a "fundamental element of the property right" *Kaiser Aetna*, 444 U. S., at 179–180, that cannot be balanced away. Our cases establish that appropriations of a right to invade are *per se* physical takings.

The majority opinion goes on from there to downplay any fears of a slippery slope problem that this ruling will endanger a much broader set of government regulations in the future. The Roberts court writes:

> unlike standard health and safety inspections, the access regulation is not germane to any benefit provided to agricultural employers or any risk posed to the public. See *Horne*, 576 U. S., at 366 ("basic and familiar uses of property" are not a special benefit that "the Government may hold hostage, to be ransomed by the waiver of constitutional protection"). The access regulation amounts to simple appropriation of private property.

We should note that different commentators will interpret the court decision and its ramifications in many different ways. A fair reading is that the court has shifted the rights, at least in this specific case of the California regulations, to a Hohfeldian right to the agricultural employers to exclude the union organizers and a duty on those organizers to stay off the employer's property. A first-order analysis would indicate that perhaps we will observe fewer union members and more freedom to operate for agricultural employers. Given the number of briefs filed in this case, the broader employer community saw this as an important case for their own interests. The opportunity set of agricultural employers has expanded and they can impose costs, even if indirectly, on the unions. The unions have had their option or opportunity set reduced and thus the scope of mutual coercion has shifted in the economy in this case.

The dissent authored by Justice Breyer takes the view that a right given to a union to temporarily and under specific restrictions enter an employer's property is not a per se or physical taking. Breyer and the minority emphasize that their opinion is based on U.S. practice and their view of status quo law. Breyer writes:

> But the law is clear: A regulation that provides *temporary*, not *permanent*, access to a landowner's property, and that does not amount to a taking of a traditional property interest, is not a *per se* taking. That is, it does not automatically require compensation. Rather, a court must consider whether it goes "too far."

The minority also argues that the majority opinion tries to narrow its ruling but in so doing creates a whole new range of rules and exceptions that make the issue of takings laws even more complicated. As we can observe, Supreme Court rulings are never clear cut but do provide an important check point as to how the economy will continue to evolve in the future. The court ruling in *Cedar Point* does place greater burden on farmworker unions especially in regard to migrant laborers, in their objective of providing for organization and assistance. The extent of the amicus briefs filed on the behalf of the employer

Table 7.1   *Right of entry*

	Unions	Employees	Employers
Rule 1: Union has a right to enter employer property	More union members, easier time organizing and communicating with new and existing members	Potentially improved employee wages and benefits from stronger and wider bargaining position	Higher operating costs
Rule 2: Employer has a right to exclude unions from property	Fewer members, more difficult communicating with members and higher operating costs	Potentially impact on wages and benefits	Lower operating costs, exclusion power maintained

also reveals the extent to which the business side wishes to curtail union legal power and expand its own legal power.

A rule that favors greater ease and likelihood of just compensation being paid out for a taking will be a very different world than one where the payout of just compensation is rarer and less likely to happen. The analyst could compare various institutional alternatives as laid out in Table 7.1 to determine differences in economic performance.

An empirical analysis could be done perhaps comparing California to other states with a similar agricultural sector but no access regulation law. This analysis could compare the number of union employees, agricultural wages and benefits, for example. The institutional variable would be the existence or non-existence of the access regulation.

8. Common property and fisheries management in the Northeast Canyons and Seamounts national marine area

8.1 SITUATION

In Chapter 3, we introduced the idea of common property as a type of property jointly held and managed through various formal or informal means by members of a community or going concern(s). These co-owners hold varying bundles of rights to the resource that cannot be lost through non-use. Many interesting institutional alternatives for the management of common property or common-pool resource situations have been explored throughout time.

Historically, common-pool resources have been managed through both formal and informal systems of common property. As described by Ciriacy-Wantrup and Bishop (1975), the common ownership of natural resources in communal hunting and gathering societies provide perhaps the earliest examples. Throughout much of the history of Great Britain to the present, grazing of livestock on common land was seasonal and managed through controls such as feed requirements (equal to the amount necessary to sustain livestock during non-grazing hours), scheduling (seasonally appropriate and daylight hours only) and in some cases via the assignment of quotas limiting the number of animals the common users could graze on the area (Ciriacy-Wantrup and Bishop, 1975). Common forest lands on the European continent provide similar examples. In each of these cases, some form of governance was occurring whether it be formal or informal in an institutional context.

Fisheries, often considered a classic case of a common-pool good, are no exception. According to Ciriacy-Wantrup and Bishop (1975):

> Riparian institutions regulated the use of water from surface streams in England and on the continent long before formal riparian law was developed in Anglo-Saxon common law and German land law. The notion that the users of a common surface source were co-equal in right was anchored in customs and traditions long before a codified and legally enforceable riparian law existed. One of the factors favorable to this development was the long experience with the commons in grazing and forest resources.

In the modern era, the concept of common property is already at work in managing groundwater and fisheries. Over the course of the last several decades, the importance of good stewardship of fisheries and aquaculture resources has become more widely understood and prioritized. The state of marine resources, however, has continued to decline. According to the Food and Agriculture Organization (2020), the proportion of fish stocks that are within biologically sustainable levels has fallen from 90 percent in 1974 to 65.8 percent in 2017. This degradation of fish stock is often attributed to a lack of strong management as well as issues with enforcement of existing rule structures, such as in the use of total allowable catch for a given year (Beddington et al., 2007). One example of an institutional alternative at work in some areas is the creation of rights-based incentives for fishermen or rights-based fisheries reforms, such as through the use of individual transferable quotas.

Management of common-pool resources like fisheries is one area where traditional ideas of property rights and rules become particularly muddled. Nobel Laureate Elinor Ostrom did a great deal of work in considering the institutional alternatives for managing common-pool resources. Given the background of common property regarding fisheries management above, we can begin to reimagine some of Ostrom's property types by their Hohfeldian counterparts. The analysis here is not intended to be exhaustive, but rather to serve as an example for how to begin thinking of issues of rights when there is no clear legal case or doctrine to guide you.

Briefly, Ostrom believed that there were institutional alternatives other than simply market versus central control. In her Nobel speech, Ostrom focused on moving away from the classic public versus private goods dichotomy and challenged us to think about the "subtractability of use" and a "difficulty of exclusion," particularly in prescribing governance systems for common-pool resources or goods (Ostrom, 2010). These goods were typically defined as one where exclusion was difficult for multiple users, but that each user's consumption reduced the total goods available for all. This is in contrast to a pure public good where exclusion is generally very difficult, and one user's consumption does not reduce other users' consumption. The existence of these characteristics becomes important in understanding the performance of various institutional alternatives.

Ostrom observed that communities often found ways to address these common-pool resource problems and avoid the tragedy of the commons. Of particular importance, Ostrom emphasized that the ability to exclude was only one facet of property rights and that a whole series of other rights was present (see, for instance, Schlager and Ostrom, 1992). This is in keeping with the bundle-of-rights approach discussed briefly in Chapter 3. For instance, communities could find ways to manage common-pool resources through a certain bundle of rights that may include managing withdrawal rights, even if the ability to exclude was not included.

Ostrom's observation that local communities do find ways to overcome the problem of commons management (and the large body of work that followed) does not imply that this approach will always work or does always work (or even whether we can define what "works" means in this context), but rather that the analyst should consider all alternatives where possible. In the situation of common-pool goods and fisheries specifically, the interdependence between economic agents takes on both a biological and physical form. The fact that these resources are needed for the biological well being of humanity implies an almost infinite number of stakeholders, while the physical reality that exclusion is hard in these cases means that different sets of institutional alternatives may need to be considered by the analyst. To this point, we consider institutional alternatives in a conflict involving marine management of an area off the coast of Cape Cod, Massachusetts in the following sections.

8.1.1   Legal Background

In 2016, President Obama designated a portion of the Atlantic Ocean off the coast of Cape Cod, Massachusetts as a national marine sanctuary. The area was designated as the Northeast Canyons and Seamounts marine national monument to protect "distinct geological features" and "unique ecological resources" in the northern Atlantic Ocean (Proclamation No. 9496, 3 C.F.R. 262, 262 (2017)). This move created conflict with local commercial interests, banning both commercial fishing (outside of a seven-year exception for the harvesting of certain marine species) and drilling. In Hohfeldian terms, lobstermen and other fishing entities were placed under a Hohfeldian duty not to fish in those areas. The Hohfeldian right was held by the citizens of the U.S. (and arguably other nations as well given the nature of the ocean in the ecosystem).

In response to this monument designation, the fishing industry filed a lawsuit against the Secretary of Commerce Wilbur Ross in 2017 (in charge of the National Atmospheric and Oceanic Administration which oversees the regulations). In *Massachusetts Lobstermen's Association* v. *Ross* (2019), the lobstermen and fishermen industries were seeking permanent injunction and declaratory relief against fishing regulations in the monument area. This permanent injunction would mean that the federal government could not enact fishing regulations through the national monument process.

The plaintiffs had their case dismissed in the federal district court. They then appealed to the federal appeals court and lost and then appealed again to the U.S. Supreme Court. The Supreme Court denied taking up the case in 2021. Chief Justice Roberts wrote the denial stating that the case did not meet the criteria the court has set to accept such cases, although also stating that the court was not ruling on the merits in the case (529 U.S. 2021). This means that the current status quo rules remain in place and the fishermen and lobstermen remain under a Hohfeldian duty to refrain from operating within the monument area.

During this same period, President Trump issued executive orders which impacted the marine monument in 2017. In 2020, President Trump allowed commercial fishing to resume in the marine monument area but did not allow drilling. In 2021 President Biden rescinded the Trump-era executive orders and placed the issue under investigation (NRDC, 2021).

8.2   INSTITUTIONAL ALTERNATIVES AND CONSIDERATIONS

Analysts and governments have been seeking alternative institutional regimes in oceans and other fisheries settings. The fisheries situation is of interest not only in its own right but also because the theory of common property resources traces its origins to the literature on fisheries economics. Overfishing has occurred with increasing frequency over the last century (Food and Agriculture Organization, 2020). The bulk of the literature blames this problem on the common property condition, particularly the issue of the market failure due to the inability to exclude producers. At the same time, this market-based approach to the overfishing problem of assigning property rights has been criticized for failing to see the multitude of problems that actually exist in real fisheries (Young et al., 2018). Moreover, given the historical context of common-pool resources, it is apparent that the issue has never been whether there are property rights present or not, but rather to whom they are given and exactly what they include.

For the purpose of considering relevant institutional alternatives, it is useful to consider the legal or institutional context prior to the present situation and in other similar sectors or resource areas in both a geographic and historical context. Prior to the designation of Georges Bank as a national marine monument, the area's management primarily fell under the purview of the Magnuson-Stevens Fishery Conservation and Management Act (MSFA). The MSFA, passed by Congress in 1976, is the primary law regulating marine fisheries management in U.S. federal waters. This is done through regional management councils for various marine areas and a set of national standards to balance the economic interests of fishing along with environmental and wildlife protection interests. These regional councils set fishing limits and establish overall fish management plans based on scientific evidence and research.

The MSFA did many things, including extending U.S. sea rights from 12 nautical miles from the coast to 200 miles from the coast. This rule was later adopted by the United Nations as part of internal law. This created a Hohfeldian right to the U.S. and a Hohfeldian duty for other nations and their fishing fleets to stay out of U.S. waters. The U.S. retained the legal power to potentially negotiate permission to operate in U.S. waters (and the same for other countries).

Following the MSFA's passage, Georges Bank and the area that is currently the marine monument (amongst many others) were significantly restructured in terms of institutional makeup. The fishermen and lobstermen, within the limits prescribed by the local council, had a Hohfeldian protected privilege to operate. They were protected in that other agents were not allowed to interfere with their operations. One could even argue that it was a protected liberty in that fishermen could decide to operate or not operate as economic conditions and other factors impacted their decision making.

The MSFA also structured enforcement or secondary jural or legal relations. The MSFA is enforced on behalf of the U.S. by the National Oceanic and Atmospheric Administration Office of Law Enforcement along with other law enforcement agencies at the state and local levels. This agency covers thousands of miles of ocean and coastal areas, has 200 staff and a budget of just over $70 million.

Prior to the passage of the MSFA, there appeared to be a lack of community-based management systems in the Georges Bank fishing area for some time (Verani, 2007). According to both academic literature and media reports, the region was heavily fished by many different fleets besides the American one (American Museum of Natural History, n.d.). This wide dispersal of fishing fleets may have generated a significant number of barriers to local or community solutions of the kind that Ostrom found in other common-pool resource situations. By many accounts, it appears that any locally devised solutions to address the commons problem in this fishing region had either been non-existent or had broken down over time.

In 2016, the relevant institutional landscape was again reshaped as discussed earlier in this chapter. President Obama used the Federal Antiquities Act and the Federal Monument Act to reshape the legal economic nexus. A significant portion of this northeast fishing region and the Georges Bank was designated as a national marine monument, the first of its kind. This designation went beyond fishing and prevented other economic activities such as drilling in that same area. It exerted new duties on a number of economic producers. In the executive order, President Obama did provide a seven-year period where some fishing could continue. This designation was the starting point for the lobstermen's lawsuit.

There are several institutional options that may be available and should be investigated in this situation. In this case, the relevant institutional alternatives besides the current one may include: (1) central control of a strict quota system; (2) a transferable quota system that uses a form of market; (3) no organized form or informal limit or quota system; and (4) blocked exchanges or legal prohibitions on any commercial fishing activity in a specific area. Each of these institutional alternatives would need to be classified into a Hohfeldian understanding of the legal framework. From there, a first- and second-order economic analysis can be conducted. Again, the court case provides a sense of some institutional alternatives, but one can also pull from the academic research and investigations from other fisheries around the world.

One institutional option is the use of quantitatively defined "quotas" for fisheries that may be transferable or non-transferable (Vatn, 2018). The research indicates that a transferable quota may be more effective in protecting fish stocks but also that these tend to be concentrated in a small number of operators. There is a growing chorus that this institutional approach has its weaknesses as well, especially when dealing in certain ocean ecosystems (Vatn, 2018). A quota system provides a Hohfeldian right, within limits, where operators can function while others have a duty not to interfere. However, there are baseline questions as to how these rights are distributed and how we deal with new versus existing operators. Are new potential operators under a duty not to transact or try to enter the market? If there are transferable quotes, what are the legal rules and how do legal powers get distributed under such a system? Do certain arrangements lead to a concentration of market and economic power in certain agents? There is also the relative question of whether this is the best strategy and especially "best" in the context of the distribution of gains and losses. Other institutional options may provide different performance outcomes for various stakeholders. These are the questions that can drive a research agenda with the Hohfeldian scheme.

An empirical impact analysis might focus on the distributional income and wealth consequences for fishing groups (both recreational and commercial), environmental interests and concerns, wildlife and marine animals and other impacted consumers and producers. To understand the implications of various institutional structures, one could examine various countries and places where the rules vary from one to another.

8.3   FURTHER NOTES

To emphasize further a point from Chapter 1, the various institutional alternatives in the case of the Northeast Canyons would all lead to an economically efficient outcome. Presuming an acceptance of the standard neoclassical economics behavioral model, economic agents will respond to changes in the institutional environment and the changes in price signals to operate in a new optimal manner. Production and technological efficiency will be achieved. Those efficiency points may not be desirable for industry participants from the standpoint of overall profitability – but that is a separate question. The economically efficient point also does not address any environmental or other ecological sustainability questions. In the case when an analyst is relying on more complex behavioral assumptions such as those suggested by institutional economist Thorstein Veblen or more recent authors including Richard Thaler and Danny Kahneman, the very notion of economic efficiency becomes muddled (Ogaki and Tanaka, 2017).

We provided some potential institutional alternatives to consider using LEP in the case of the Northeast Canyons and Seamounts national marine area in this chapter, but these alternatives are unlikely to become reality without significant political backing. Should the issue come before the courts, existing law and legal interpretation is likely to have more impact on decision making than some perceived view of economic efficiency.

Moreover, in the case of environmental issues, concepts of cost and who bears it become especially complicated. Overfishing today means less fish for the producers and consumers of tomorrow. Similarly, the pollution or waste created by production today that may not be priced in for the producer doesn't simply cease to exist. Institutions may be structured so that the cost of cleanup or disposal of x good, or the impacts of a firms overfishing are not born by the producer, but that simply means they will be borne elsewhere. Institutional changes in this sphere directly impact how these costs are distributed, who bears them and when (and which efficient point is chosen). A cost avoided by a consumer today may be borne by another tomorrow, and whether we think this is fair or economical or the efficient will of the market depends on the way we set up the rules, or institutions, that guide our interactions. LEP can help us examine the rules and their context more closely to consider the numerous possibilities there are for dealing with human interdependence in these cases and get at the root of what is being gained and lost by all stakeholders.

9. Conclusion: Themes from Legal-Economic Performance

The economy and economic performance is a complex mix of millions of individuals and institutions around the world making daily decisions on investments, consumption, production and allocation of resources that result in income flows, asset values, debt levels and many other variables. Traditionally, economists have thought about how these dynamics are driven by consumer preferences, production technology, budget constraints and the prices of inputs, outputs, substitutes and complements across these economic agents. At the same time, there have been groups of economists and other experts such as lawyers, sociologists and economic agents themselves who recognized that human-created formal and informal rules play an important role in shaping the decision-making process.

In this text, we join the ranks of those that acknowledge that institutions, and more specifically the law, cannot be separated from the study of economics. All economic agents are tied together in a legal system given the inherent interdependent nature of transactions in a complex global economy. Standard neoclassical models and approaches may treat the legal framework all economic actors operate in as exogenous to the model in the interest of ease of use and, often, necessity. But these assumptions, their limitations and parameters must be well understood. When we conduct any economic analysis, especially micro-institutional impact analysis, without domain knowledge about the operationalization of variables, mechanisms, etc., we run the risk of drawing misleading conclusions at best and useless or damaging conclusions at worst.

The reality is that in every institutional setting, the government (law) and market (or private participants) are always involved. Framing alternatives as community versus market or individual versus government is not helpful or informative. Each alternative is a mix of these things as emphasized by the term Legal-Economic Performance (or Warren Samuels' legal–economic nexus). When we focus on framing the institutional alternatives as a complex mix of economic agents, incentives and legal and informal rules, we more accurately specify what is happening in a conflict and can begin to more fully understand outcomes (and even potential feedbacks). We recognize that rules, of both a formal form or of informal or cultural form, shape the opportunity sets and options that consumers, producers and other economic agents (including governments) can act from (Chapter 1). They take the form of both enablements and disablements for various economic agents and actions as rights, duties, privilege, exposure and as power, liability, disability, immunity and compound relations (Chapters 2 and 3). In other words, institutions enable and expand the opportunity set of some agents while simultaneously restricting the opportunity set of other agents.

Analysts can use the tools and language in this book to explore, investigate and assess the institutional alternatives that are available to address interdependence in the economy. These structural options exist everywhere. Labor relations between management and employees is structured by a whole series of laws whether they involve labor unions or not. Consumers and retailers/ producers are implicitly or explicitly invoking legal forms as they exchange goods and services both during and after the transaction. Housing markets and real property are guided in most countries by a whole series of legal traditions and rules as buyers and sellers interact. Agricultural and food systems are governed by formal and informal rules regarding the delivery and quality of products, standardization and weight measurement and pricing. Not all economic analysis directly involves examining institutional alternatives, but these factors are at least in the background in every sector and every country in one form or another. In some countries, the rules may be more informal than formal, and enforcement may vary, but even these conditions act as a type of institutional structure.

We wrote this text to provide analysts and students with a set of tools and a language for examining and understanding the legal foundations of the economy. Rather than determine the optimal set of laws or other institutions, we encourage students and analysts to understand the impact of the laws as they exist on economic performance and the distribution of income, wealth and resources. We call this the Legal-Economic Performance framework (Chapter 4). Court cases and judicial activity provide a useful, albeit not the only, source of data for using this toolkit. Methods for measuring performance can be both qualitative and quantitative.

Our LEP approach to impact analysis is distinct from a traditional law and economics approach in two ways. One is that we do not presuppose that all human behavior is founded on rational choice. There are now a wide range of behavioral models that can be used to explore the first- and second-order implications of each institutional alternative. Institutional economists have explored many of these models going all the way back to Thorstein Veblen and his focus on the power of social traditions and history driving human decision making.

The second distinction is that we rely on the idea that all presumed neutral or objective choice criteria such as economic efficiency are based on a normative foundation. Each institutional alternative is examined as a Pareto-efficient

allocation of resources in and of itself and cannot be compared using efficiency against one another. Explicit value judgments must be used in deciding
between each institutional alternative.

This approach contrasts sharply with those that seek an "optimal" institution
or ignore institutions altogether in pursuit of economic efficiency. Economics
has a long-stated tradition of using efficiency to compare states of the economy
and examining a potential trade-off between the distribution of prices in the
concept of equity and efficiency. The approach embodied in LEP is based
on the idea that economic efficiency is a normative criterion like any other
and infers a set of stated or unstated normative values. If the analyst is using
economic efficiency or a similar criterion, it needs to be done in the context
of a specifically stated and transparent set of normative values. Otherwise, the
analyst should stick to the presentation of a wide range of economic performance variables and allow the relevant going concern to use their processes
for choice.

We do not provide guidance on such choice here. Rather, we provide
researchers with basic legal concepts and tools to apply in various analyses
through the LEP framework and leave you with the question: whose interests
count?

Appendix A: *Miller v. Schoene*

Petitioner	Respondent
Miller	Schoene
Decided	**Decided by**
February 20, 1928	Taft Court
Advocates	**Case numbers**
N/A	Docket no.: 199
	Citation: 276 US 272 (1928)

FACTS OF THE CASE

Miller owned a large stand of ornamental red cedar trees on his property in Shenandoah County, Virginia. Schoene, the Virginia state entomologist, ordered Miller to cut down his red cedar trees pursuant to the Cedar Rust Act of Virginia. Miller's property was near an apple orchard, and Virginia did not want the cedar rust plant disease to spread from Miller's trees to the apple orchard. The state provided no compensation for destroying the red cedars. Miller alleged that this was a government taking requiring compensation and that the Cedar Rust Act violated the due process clause. The Virginia courts upheld the tree removal order.

QUESTION

Did Virginia's Cedar Rust Act violate the due process clause of the Fourteenth Amendment?

CONCLUSION

In a unanimous decision, the court upheld Virginia's statute and the order to remove Miller's cedar trees. A unanimous decision by Justice Harlan Stone found that the statute and the order to remove Miller's cedar trees did not violate the due process clause. The court recognized the state's interest in preventing the cedar rust from damaging nearby apple orchards as they were the "principal agriculture pursuit" in the state. The court held that the destruction of Miller's trees would be a taking of his property; however, the state "did not exceed its constitutional powers by deciding upon the destruction of one class of property in order to save another which, in the judgment of the legislature, is of greater value to the public." In sum, the legislature acted reasonably in determining that apples were more valuable to the state's interests than red cedar.

ATTRIBUTION

Case summaries are provided by Oyez (www.oyez.org), a free law project by Justia and the Legal Information Institute of Cornell Law School.

Appendix B: *Masterpiece Cakeshop v. Colorado CRC*

Petitioner	**Respondent**
Masterpiece Cakeshop, Ltd.	Colorado Civil Rights Commission, Charlie Craig and David Mullins
Decided	**Decided by**
June 4, 2018	Roberts Court
Advocates	**Case numbers**
Kristen Kellie Waggoner: for petitioners	Docket no.: 16-111
Noel J. Francisco: Solicitor General, U.S.	Citation: 584 US (2018)
Department of Justice, for the U.S. as amicus curiae	
supporting petitioners	
Frederick R. Yarger: for state respondents	
David D. Cole: for private respondents	

FACTS OF THE CASE

In July 2012, Charlie Craig and David Mullins went to Masterpiece Cakeshop in Lakewood, Colorado, and requested that its owner, Jack C. Phillips, design and create a cake for their wedding. Phillips declined to do so on the grounds that he does not create wedding cakes for same-sex weddings because of his religious beliefs. Phillips believes that decorating cakes is a form of art through which he can honor God and that it would displease God to create cakes for same-sex marriages.

Craig and Mullins filed charges of discrimination with the Colorado Civil Rights Division, alleging discrimination based on sexual orientation under the Colorado Anti-Discrimination Act (CADA), §§ 24-34-301 to 804, C.R.S. 2014. After the division issued a notice of determination finding probable cause, Craig and Mullins filed a formal complaint with the Office of Administrative Courts alleging that Masterpiece discriminated against them in a place of public accommodation in violation of CADA.

The administrative law judge issued a written order finding in favor of Craig and Mullins, which was affirmed by the Colorado Civil Rights Commission.

On appeal, the Colorado Court of Appeals subsequently affirmed the commission's ruling.

QUESTION

Does the application of Colorado's public accommodations law to compel a cakemaker to design and make a cake that violates his sincerely held religious beliefs about same-sex marriage violate the free speech or free exercise clauses of the First Amendment?

CONCLUSION

7–2 Decision for Masterpiece Cakeshop, Ltd.
Majority opinion by Anthony M. Kennedy

The court reversed in a 7–2 decision, holding that the Colorado Civil Rights Commission's conduct in evaluating a cakeshop owner's reasons for declining to make a wedding cake for a same-sex couple violated the free exercise clause.

The court explained that while gay persons and same-sex couples are afforded civil rights protections under the laws and the Constitution, religious and philosophical objections to same-sex marriage are protected views and can also be protected forms of expression. The Colorado law at issue in this case, which prohibited discrimination against gay people in purchasing products and services, had to be applied in a neutral manner with regard to religion. The majority acknowledged that from Phillips' perspective, creating cakes was a form of artistic expression and a component of his sincere religious beliefs.

The court also explained that in 2012, the year that Phillips refused his services to Craig and Mullins, the law in Colorado and across the country with regard to same-sex marriage was much more unsettled than it became after *United States* v. *Windsor*, 570 US 744 (2013) and *Obergefell* v. *Hodges*, 576 US (2015). At the time, the State Civil Rights Division had also concluded in at least three other cases that bakers had acted lawfully in declining to make cakes that included messages they disagreed with, specifically messages demeaning gay persons. Thus it was not unreasonable for Phillips to believe that he was acting lawfully at the time, and his claims before the commission were entitled to neutral treatment.

However, the court stated that Phillips did not receive this neutral treatment, with members of the commission showing clear and impermissible hostility toward his religious beliefs. The court explained that commissioners' comments disparaging Phillips' beliefs and characterizing them as rhetorical were inappropriate, though these comments were not mentioned or disavowed in subsequent legal proceedings. The court concluded that these comments cast doubt on the fairness of the commission's consideration of Phillips' claims. The court also pointed out that disparities between Phillips' case and those of other bakers with objections to making cakes with anti-gay messages, and who were victorious before the commission, further reflected hostility toward the religious basis for Phillips' position.

The court concluded that the commission's actions violated the state's duty under the First Amendment not to use hostility toward religion or a religious viewpoint as a basis for laws or regulations. Under the facts of this case, the court determined that Phillips' religious justification for his refusal to serve Craig and Mullins was not afforded the neutral treatment mandated by the free exercise clause.

Justice Ginsburg authored a dissenting opinion, in which she was joined by Justice Sotomayor, stating that neither the commission's comments regarding Phillips' religious views nor its alleged disparate treatment of bakers objecting to making cakes with anti-gay messages justified ruling in favor of Phillips.

Justice Kagan filed a concurring opinion, joined by Justice Breyer, in which she agreed with the majority that the commission had not given neutral treatment to Phillips' religious views, but declined to assign any significance to the commission's treatment of bakers who refused to create cakes with anti-gay messages because she believed that this did not violate the Colorado law at issue in Phillips' case.

Justice Gorsuch also filed a concurring opinion, joined by Justice Alito, in which he argued that the cases of Phillips and the bakers who objected to using anti-gay messages in their baking were quite similar, and the commission acted inappropriately in treating them differently.

Justice Thomas filed an opinion concurring in part and concurring in the judgment and was joined by Justice Gorsuch. Thomas argued that an order requiring Phillips to bake a wedding cake for a same-sex couple would violate his First Amendment rights.

ATTRIBUTION

Case summaries are provided by Oyez (www.oyez.org), a free law project by Justia and the Legal Information Institute of Cornell Law School.

Appendix C: *Lochner v. New York*

Petitioner	Respondent
Joseph Lochner	New York
Decided	**Decided by**
April 17, 1905	Fuller Court
Advocates	**Case numbers**
Henry Weismann: for Lochner pro hoc vice	Docket no.: 292
Frank Harvey Field: for Lochner	Citation: 198 US 45 (1905)
J. M. Meyer: for New York	

FACTS OF THE CASE

The state of New York enacted a statute known as the Bakeshop Act, which forbid bakers to work more than 60 hours a week or 10 hours a day. Lochner was accused of permitting an employee to work more than 60 hours in one week. The first charge resulted in a fine of $25, and a second charge a few years later resulted in a fine of $50. While Lochner did not challenge his first conviction, he appealed the second, but was denied in state court. Before the Supreme Court, he argued that the Fourteenth Amendment should have been interpreted to contain the freedom to contract among the rights encompassed by substantive due process.

QUESTION

Does the Bakeshop Act violate the liberty protected by the due process clause of the Fourteenth Amendment?

CONCLUSION

5–4 decision for Lochner
Majority opinion by Rufus Peckham

The New York law violated "liberty of contract" protected by the due process clause of the Fourteenth Amendment.

The court invalidated the New York law. The majority maintained that the statute interfered with the freedom of contract, and thus the Fourteenth Amendment's right to liberty afforded to employer and employee. The court further held that the New York law failed the rational basis test for determining whether government action is constitutional. The majority reasoned that the Bakeshop Act had no rational basis because long working hours did not dramatically undermine the health of employees, and baking is not particularly dangerous.

Broadly interpreting state authority to regulate under its police powers, Justice Harlan in his dissent articulated reasoning that would inform later decisions in the post-*Lochner* era. Rather than requiring the government to prove that a law had a rational basis, he would require the party challenging the law to prove that the test was not met. (This is the current rule.)

ATTRIBUTION

Case summaries are provided by Oyez (www.oyez.org), a free law project by Justia and the Legal Information Institute of Cornell Law School.

Appendix D: *TransUnion LLC v. Ramirez*

Petitioner	Respondent
TransUnion LLC	Sergio L. Ramirez
Decided	**Decided by**
June 25, 2021	Roberts Court
Advocates	**Case numbers**
Paul D. Clement: for the petitioner	Docket no.: 20-297
Nicole F. Reaves: for the U.S., as amicus curiae,	Citation: 594 US (2021)
supporting neither party	
Samuel Issacharoff: for the respondent	

FACTS OF THE CASE

In February 2011, Sergio Ramirez went with his wife and father-in-law to purchase a car. When the dealership ran a joint credit check on Ramirez and his wife, it discovered that Ramirez was on a list maintained by the Treasury Department's Office of Foreign Assets Control (OFAC), of people with whom U.S. companies cannot do business (i.e. "a terrorist list"). Ramirez and his wife still bought a car that day, but they purchased it in her name only. TransUnion, the company that had prepared the report, eventually removed the OFAC alert from any future credit reports that might be requested by or for Ramirez.

On behalf of himself and others similarly situated, Ramirez sued TransUnion in federal court, alleging that the company's actions violated the Fair Credit Reporting Act. The district court certified a class of everyone who, during a six-month period, had received a letter from TransUnion stating that their name was a "potential match" for one on the OFAC list, although only a fraction of those class members had their credit reports sent to a third party.

The jury awarded each class member nearly $1,000 for violations of the Fair Credit Reporting Act and over $6,000 in punitive damages, for a total verdict of over $60 million. On appeal, the U.S. Court of Appeals for the Ninth Circuit upheld the statutory damages but reduced the punitive damages to approximately $32 million.

TransUnion asked the Supreme Court to resolve two questions, of which the court agreed to decide only the first.

QUESTION

Does either Article III of the Constitution or Federal Rule of Civil Procedure 23 permit a damages class action when the majority of the class did not suffer an injury comparable to that of the class representative?

CONCLUSION

5–4 decision for TransUnion
Majority opinion by Brett M. Kavanaugh

Only a plaintiff concretely harmed by a defendant's violation of the Fair Credit Reporting Act has Article III standing to seek damages against that private defendant in federal court. Justice Brett Kavanaugh authored the 5–4 majority opinion.

To have Article III standing to sue in federal court, a plaintiff must show that she suffered concrete injury in fact, that the injury was fairly traceable to the defendant's conduct and that the injury is likely to be redressed by a favorable ruling by the court. To show a concrete injury, a plaintiff must demonstrate that the asserted harm is similar to a harm traditionally recognized as providing a basis for a lawsuit in American courts – i.e. a close historical or common-law analogue for their asserted injury.

Of the 8,185 class members, TransUnion provided third parties with credit reports containing OFAC alerts for only 1,853 individuals; these individuals have standing. The remaining 6,332 class members stipulated that TransUnion did not provide their credit information to any potential creditors during the designated class period and thus failed to demonstrate the concrete harm required for Article III standing. Mere risk of future harm is insufficient to establish standing.

Justice Clarence Thomas authored a dissenting opinion, joined by Justices Stephen Breyer, Sonia Sotomayor and Elena Kagan. Justice Thomas argued that injury in law to a private right has historically been sufficient to establish "injury in fact" for standing purposes, and each class member in this case has demonstrated violation of their private rights.

Justice Kagan authored a dissenting opinion joined by Justices Breyer and Sotomayor arguing that Congress expressly allowed these plaintiffs to bring their claim of violation of the Fair Credit Reporting Act, yet the majority disallows them from doing so. Justice Kagan noted her slightly different understanding of the "concrete injury" requirement for Article III standing that

Justice Thomas described in his dissent but suggested such a difference would not lead to a different outcome.

ATTRIBUTION

Case summaries are provided by Oyez (www.oyez.org), a free law project by Justia and the Legal Information Institute of Cornell Law School.

Appendix E: *Cedar Point Nursery v. Hassid*

Petitioner	Respondent
Cedar Point Nursery et al.	Victoria Hassid et al.
Decided	**Decided by**
June 23, 2021	Roberts Court
Advocates	**Case numbers**
Joshua P. Thompson: for the petitioners	Docket no.: 20-107
Michael J. Mongan: for the respondents	Citation: 594 US (2021)

FACTS OF THE CASE

In 1975, California enacted the Agricultural Labor Relations Act (ALRA), which, among other things, created the Agricultural Labor Relations Board ("the Board"). Shortly after the ALRA went into effect and established the Board, the Board promulgated a regulation allowing union organizers access to agricultural employees at employer worksites under specific circumstances.

Cedar Point Nursery, an Oregon corporation, operates a nursery in Dorris, California, that raises strawberry plants for producers. It employs approximately 100 full-time workers and more than 400 seasonal workers at that location. On October 29, 2015, organizers from the United Farm Workers union (UFW) entered the nursery, without providing prior written notice of intent to take access as required by the regulation. The UFW allegedly disrupted the workers, and some workers left their work stations to join the protest, while a majority of workers did not.

Sometime later, the UFW served Cedar Point with written notice of intent to take access. Cedar Point filed a charge against the UFW with the Board, alleging that the UFW had violated the access regulation by failing to provide the required written notice before taking access. The UFW likewise filed a counter-charge, alleging that Cedar Point had committed an unfair labor practice.

Cedar Point then sued the Board in federal district court alleging that the access regulation, as applied to them, amounted to a taking without compensation, in violation of the Fifth Amendment, and an illegal seizure, in violation of the Fourth Amendment. The district court granted the Board's motion to dismiss for failure to state a claim, and Cedar Point appealed. Reviewing the district court's order granting the motion to dismiss de novo, the U.S. Court of Appeals for the Ninth Circuit concluded that the access regulation did not violate either provision, and it affirmed the lower court.

QUESTION

Does the California regulation granting labor organizations a "right to take access" to an agricultural employer's property to solicit support for unionization constitute a per se physical taking under the Fifth Amendment?

CONCLUSION

6–3 decision for Cedar Point Nursery
Majority opinion by John G. Roberts, Jr.

The California regulation granting labor organizations a "right to take access" to an agricultural employer's property to solicit support for unionization constitutes a per se physical taking. Chief Justice John Roberts authored the 6–3 majority opinion of the court.

The takings clause of the Fifth Amendment of the U.S. Constitution, which applies to the states via the Fourteenth Amendment, prohibits the government from taking private property for public use "without just compensation." There are two types of takings: physical appropriations of land and imposition of regulations that restrict the landowner's ability to use the land. Physical takings must be compensated. Use restrictions are evaluated using a flexible test developed in *Penn Central Transportation Co.* v. *New York City*, 438 U.S. 104 (1978), which balances factors such as the "economic impact of the regulation, its interference with reasonable investment-backed expectations, and the character of the government action."

In this case, the California regulation granting labor organizations a "right to take access" to an agricultural employer's property is a physical taking. The regulation does not restrict the growers' use of their own property, but instead appropriates the owners' right to exclude third parties from their land, "one of the most treasured rights" of property ownership. By granting access to third-party union organizers, even for a limited time, the regulation confers a right to physically invade the growers' property and thus constitutes a physical taking.

Justice Brett Kavanaugh authored a concurring opinion describing another way the court could have arrived at the same conclusion, using a different precedent.

Justice Stephen Breyer authored a dissenting opinion, in which Justices Sonia Sotomayor and Elena Kagan joined. Justice Breyer argued that the regulation does not physically appropriate growers' property; rather, it temporarily regulates their right to exclude others and as such should be subject to the "flexible" Penn Central rule.

ATTRIBUTION

Case summaries are provided by Oyez (www.oyez.org), a free law project by Justia and the Legal Information Institute of Cornell Law School.

Appendix F: *Roberts v. United States Jaycees*

Petitioner	Respondent
Roberts	United States Jaycees
Decided	**Decided by**
July 3, 1984	Burger Court
Advocates	**Case numbers**
Richard L. Varco, Jr.: argued the cause for the appellants	Docket no.: 83-724
	Citation: 468 US 609 (1984)
Carl D. Hall, Jr.: argued the cause for the appellee	

FACTS OF THE CASE

According to its bylaws, membership in the United States Jaycees was limited to males between the ages of 18 and 35. Females and older males were limited to associate membership in which they were prevented from voting or holding local or national office. Two chapters of the Jaycees in Minnesota, contrary to the bylaws, admitted women as full members. When the national organization revoked the chapters' licenses, they filed a discrimination claim under a Minnesota anti-discrimination law. The national organization brought a lawsuit against Kathryn Roberts of the Minnesota Department of Human Rights, who was responsible for the enforcement of the anti-discrimination law.

QUESTION

Did Minnesota's attempts to enforce the anti-discrimination law violate the Jaycees' right to free association under the First Amendment?

CONCLUSION

Unanimous decision for Roberts
Majority opinion by William J. Brennan, Jr.

In a unanimous decision, the court held that the Jaycees' chapters lacked "the distinctive characteristics that might afford constitutional protection to the decision of its members to exclude women." The court reasoned that making women full members would not impose any serious burdens on the male members' freedom of expressive association. The court thus held that Minnesota's compelling interest in eradicating discrimination against women justified enforcement of the state anti-discrimination law. The court found that the Minnesota law was not aimed at the suppression of speech and did not discriminate on the basis of viewpoint.

ATTRIBUTION

Case summaries are provided by Oyez (www.oyez.org), a free law project by Justia and the Legal Information Institute of Cornell Law School.

Appendix G: Basic legal terminology

This is a starting point for an economic analyst to explore terms commonly used in court cases and other judicial activity.

amicus curiae	Latin term meaning "friend of the court," a situation where a party that is not a direct participant in a case files a brief for one side or the other
brief	Written legal argument submitted by petitioners in a case based on arguments as to why their side should prevail on a particular point
chattel	Property that can be moved or transported, also known as personal property
civil law system	Generally speaking, a system where written statutes are the predominant form of lawmaking (idealized; most real systems are a mixture)
coercive remedies	Requiring a Hohfeldian duty to do or not do something of a losing party
common law system	Generally speaking, judicial written opinions are a key form of lawmaking (idealized; most real systems are a mixture)
complaint	A legal document stating the facts and legal theories supporting one party's claim against another party
consideration	A benefit that is being entered into in exchange for something valuable
contract	An agreement between two or more persons regarding the intention to provide a benefit in return for a benefit
damages	Amount of money or compensation that is awarded to a complaining party against another in a lawsuit
damnum absque injuria	"Damages without injury"; a person causes damages to another person or entity without causing injury
declaratory judgement	An agent wins a court case but no damages or coercive remedies are awarded
defendant	The agent sued in a civil action or accused of a crime
dismissal	The end of a claim without any further hearings
dismissal with prejudice	A claim is ended on the merits and there is no future ability to seek relief
dismissal without prejudice	A claim is ended but the plaintiff can seek relief in the future if they so desire
duress	The use of force, threats or false imprisonment to compel another party to act in a way that is against their self-interest
good faith	Acting in an honest manner so as not to take advantage of another party
injunction (permanent and temporary)	An order issued by a court to stop conduct or activity from continuing or beginning

injury	Harm done to a person through an act or lack of an act by another party that can include tangible and intangible impacts
justiciable	Means that the case before a court has merits to be heard by that court
mandamus	A court order that a government agency do an activity or conduct
ordinance	A written law passed by a local government legislative body
plaintiff	The agents who bring a lawsuit in a civil court
property	The right to own and use a piece of land or chattel
relief	The assistance that one agent seeks from another agent in a court of law
remedy	The ability to repair a wrong or enforce a breached right
statute	A written law enacted by a state or federal legislative body
tort	A civil wrong that is not related to a breach of a voluntary contract for which some form of remedy may be available

References

A.B. 5, 2019–20 Assembly, Reg. Sess. (Cal. 2019).

American Museum of Natural History. (n.d.). The sorry story of Georges Bank. Accessed at www.amnh.org/explore/videos/biodiversity/will-the-fish-return/the -sorry-story-of-georges-bank, July 20, 2021.

Aoki, M. (2007). Endogenizing institutions and institutional changes. *Journal of Institutional Economics*, 3(1), 1–31.

Asbridge, J. (forthcoming). Redefining the boundary between regulation and appropriation. *Brigham Young University Law Review*, 47(3). https://ssrn.com/abstract= 3800341

Atkinson, G. (1990). Airspace regulation: Redefining the public domain. *Journal of Economic Issues*, 23(2), 473–480.

Atkinson, G. and Reed, M. (1990). Institutional adjustment, instrumental efficiency, and reasonable value. *Journal of Economic Issues*, 24(4), 1095–1107.

Barker, K. (2018). Private law, analytical philosophy and the modern value of Wesley Newcomb Hohfeld: A centennial appraisal. *Oxford Journal of Legal Studies*, 38(3), 585–612.

Becker, G. S. (1955). The economics of racial discrimination. Dissertation, University of Chicago.

Beddington, J. R., Agnew, D. J. and Clark, C. W. (2007). Current problems in the management of marine fisheries. *Science*, 316, 1713–1716.

Berger, B., Mapes, K. and Hicks, G. (2021). Amicus brief of legal historians in Cedar Point v. Hassid. *US Supreme Court Briefs*. https://ssrn.com/abstract=3785266

Bermeo Newcombe, C. (2017). Implied private rights of action: Definition, and factors to determine whether a private action will be implied from a federal statute. *Loyola University Chicago Law Journal*, 49, 117–147.

Bjering, E., Havro, L. J. and Moen, Ø. (2015). An empirical investigation of self-selection bias and factors influencing review helpfulness. *International Journal of Business and Management*, 10(7), 16.

Boettke, P. J. and Subrick, J. R. (2008). Does economic development require "certain" property rights? In S. S. Batie and N. Mercuro (Eds), *Alternative institutional structures: Evolution and impact* (pp. 77–90). New York: Routledge.

Brauneis, R. (1996). The foundation of our regulatory takings jurisprudence: The myth and meaning of Justice Holme's opinion in Pennsylvania Coal Co. v. Mahon. *Yale Law Journal*, 106, 613–702.

Bromley, D. W. (1989). *Economic interests and institutions: The conceptual foundations of public policy*. Oxford: Basil Blackwell.

Bromley, D. W. (1991). *Environment and economy: Property rights and public policy*. Oxford: Basil Blackwell.

Bromley, D. W. (2010). *Sufficient reason: Volitional pragmatism and the meaning of economic institutions*. Princeton, NJ: Princeton University Press.

Bromley, D. W. and Cernea M. M. (1989). The management of common property natural resources: Some conceptual and operational fallacies. *World Bank Discussion Papers*, 57.

Buchanan, J. M. (1972). Politics, property, and the law: An alternative interpretation of Miller et al. v. Schoene. *Journal of Law and Economics*, 15(2), 439–452.

Buchanan, J. M. and Samuels, W. J. (1975). On some fundamental issues in political economy: An exchange of correspondence. *Journal of Economic Issues*, 9(1), 15–38.

Burns, R. P. (1985). Blackstone's theory of the absolute rights of property. *University of Cincinnati Law Review*, 54(1), 67–86.

CA Agricultural Labor Relations Board. (2021, July 30). *Agricultural Labor Relations Board.* www.alrb.ca.gov/

Calabresi, G. and Melamed, A. D. (1972). Property rules, liability rules, and inalienability: One view of the cathedral. *Harvard Law Review*, 85(6), 1089–1128.

Chow, D. C. K. (2019). Alibaba, Amazon, and counterfeiting in the age of the internet. *Northwestern Journal of International Law and Business*, 40(2), 157–202.

Ciriacy-Wantrup, S. V. and Bishop, R. C. (1975). "Common property" as a concept in natural resources policy. *Natural Resources Journal*, 15(4), 713–727.

Coase, R. H. (1960). The problem of social cost. In *Classic papers in natural resource economics* (pp. 87–137). London: Palgrave Macmillan.

Coase, R. H. (1982). How should economists choose? In *The G. Warren Nutter lectures in political economy*. Washington, DC: American Enterprise Institute.

Coase, R. H. (1991). The institutional structure of production. The Sveriges Riksbank Prize in Economic Sciences in Memory of Alfred Nobel 1991. Accessed at www.nobelprize.org/prizes/economic-sciences/1991/coase/lecture/, November 18, 2021.

Coase, R. H. (1992). The institutional structure of production. *American Economic Review*, 82(4), 713–719.

Coase, R. H. (2012). *The firm, the market, and the law*. Chicago, IL: University of Chicago Press.

Collins, W. J. (2001). The political economy of race and the adoption of fair employment laws, 1940–1964. *NBER Historical Working Papers* 0128. National Bureau of Economic Research.

Commons, J. R. (1924). *Legal foundations of capitalism*. Piscataway, NJ: Transaction Publishers.

Commons, J. R. (1959). *Institutional economics: Its place in political economy*. Madison, WI: University of Wisconsin Press.

Cwik, B. (2016). Property rights in non-rival goods. *Journal of Political Philosophy*, 24(4), 470–486.

Denzau, A. T. and North, D. C. (2000). Shared mental models: Ideologies and institutions. In A. Lupia, M. D. McCubbins and S. L. Popkin (Eds), *Elements of reason: Cognition, choice, and the bounds of rationality* (pp. 23–46). Cambridge: Cambridge University Press.

Di Robilant, A. (2013). Property: A bundle of sticks or a tree. *Vanderbilt Law Review*, 66, 869–932.

Dynamex Operations West, Inc. v. *Superior Court*, S222732 (2018). Accessed at https://scocal.stanford.edu/opinion/dynamex-operations-west-inc-v-superior-court-34584, July 2, 2021.

Fiorito, L. (2010). John R. Commons, Wesley N. Hohfeld, and the origins of transactional economics. *History of Political Economy*, 42(2), 267–295.

Food and Agriculture Organization. (2020). The state of world fisheries and aquaculture 2020. *Sustainability in Action*. Rome. https://doi.org/10.4060/ca9229en

Friedman, M. (1953a). *Capitalism and Freedom*, 40th edition. Chicago, IL: University of Chicago Press.

Friedman, M. (1953b). The methodology of positive economics. *Essays in positive economics* (pp. 3–43). Chicago, IL: University of Chicago Press.

Friedman, M. (1962). *Capitalism and freedom: With the assistance of Rose D. Friedman*. Chicago, IL: University of Chicago Press.

Friedman, M. (1970). The social responsibility of business is to increase its profits. *New York Times Magazine*, September 13.

Garner, B. A. (2019). *Black's law dictionary*. Toronto: Thomson Reuters.

Hale, R. L. (1923). Coercion and distribution in a supposedly non-coercive state. *Political Science Quarterly*, 38(3), 470–494.

Hardin, G. (1968). The tragedy of the commons. *Science*, 162(3859), 1243–1248.

Hirschman, A. O. (1970). *Exit, voice, and loyalty: Responses to decline in firms, organizations, and states*. Cambridge, MA: Harvard University Press.

Hodgson, G. M. (1999). *Evolution and institutions: On evolutionary economics and the evolution of economics*. Cheltenham, UK and Northampton, MA, USA: Edward Elgar Publishing.

Hodgson, G. M. (2006). What are institutions? *Journal of Economic Issues*, 40(1), 1–25.

Hodgson, G. M. (2007). Evolutionary and institutional economics as the new mainstream? *Evolutionary and Institutional Economics Review*, 4(1), 7–25.

Hodgson, G. M. (2019). Taxonomic definitions in social science, with firms, markets and institutions as case studies. *Journal of Institutional Economics*, 15(2), 207–233.

Hofmann, A. W. and Mason, J. K. (2017). Amicus brief of scholars of behavioral science and economics in Masterpiece Cakeshop v. Colorado Civil Rights Commission. *SCOTUSblog*. hwww.scotusblog.com/wp-content/uploads/2017/11/16-111-bsac-Scholars-reprint.pdf

Hohfeld, W. N. (1913). Some fundamental legal conceptions as applied in judicial reasoning. *Yale Law Journal*, 23(1), 16–59.

Hohfeld, W. N. (1917). Fundamental legal conceptions as applied in judicial reasoning. *Yale Law Journal*, 26(8), 710–770.

Hohfeld, W. N. (1920). *Fundamental legal conceptions as applied in judicial reasoning: And other legal essays*. New Haven, CT: Yale University Press.

Honoré, A. M. (1961). Ownership. In A. G. Guest (Ed.), *Oxford essays in jurisprudence* (pp. 107– 147). Oxford: Oxford University Press.

Howe, A. (2021a). Court limits standing in credit-reporting lawsuit. *SCOTUSblog*. Accessed at www.scotusblog.com/2021/06/court-limits-standing-in-credit-reporting-lawsuit, November 18, 2021.

Howe, A. (2021b). Justices try to draw lines in California property-rights dispute. *SCOTUSblog*. Accessed at www.scotusblog.com/2021/03/justices-try-to-draw-lines-in-california-property-rights-dispute/, November 18, 2021.

Hu, N., Bose, I., Koh, N. S. and Liu, L. (2012). Manipulation of online reviews: An analysis of ratings, readability, and sentiments. *Decision Support Systems*, 52(3), 674–684.

Kaplowitz, M. D., Ortega-Pacheco, D. V. and Lupi, F. (2008). Payment for environmental services and other institutions for protecting drinking water in eastern Costa Rica. In S. S. Batie and N. Mercuro (Eds), *Alternative institutional structures: Evolution and impact* (pp. 380–401). London: Routledge.

Kasper, S. D. (2014). Payday lending: The case of Tennessee. *Journal of Economic Issues*, 48, 905–925.

Klammer, S. S. H., Scorsone, E. A. and Whalen, C. J. (2021). Institutional Impact Analysis: The Situation, Structure and Performance Framework. In C. Whalen (Ed), *Institutional Economics Perspectives and Methods in Pursuit of a Better World.* London: Routledge.

Komesar, N. K. (1994). *Imperfect alternatives: Choosing institutions in law, economics, and public policy.* Chicago, IL: University of Chicago Press.

Komesar, N. K. (2001). *Law's limits: The rule of law and the supply and demand of rights.* Cambridge: Cambridge University Press.

Komesar, N. K. (2008). In S. S. Batie and N. Mercuro (Eds), *Alternative institutional structures: Evolution and impact* (pp. 165–186). New York: Routledge.

Legal Information Institute. (2021, June 10). Property. Accessed at www.law.cornell .edu/wex/property, November 18, 2021.

Li, X. and Hitt, L. M. (2008). Self-selection and information role of online product reviews. *Information Systems Research*, 19(4), 456–474.

Library of Congress. (n.d.). Amdt5.5.1.1 takings clause: Overview. *Constitution Annotated.* Accessed at https://constitution.congress.gov/browse/essay/amdt5-5-1 -1/ALDE_00000920/, July 30, 2021.

MacDowell, E. L. (2014). Reimagining access to justice in the poor people's courts. *Georgetown Journal on Poverty Law and Policy*, 22(3), 473.

Massachusetts Lobstermen's Association v. *Ross*, 945 F. 3d 535 (D.C. 2019).

Masterpiece Cakeshop, Ltd. v. *Colorado Civil Rights Commission*, 138 S. Ct. 1719, 1721 (2018).

Matthews, R. C. O. (1986). The economics of institutions and the sources of growth. *The Economic Journal*, 96(384), 903–918.

McKean, M. A. (1992). Success on the commons: A comparative examination of institutions for common property resource management. *Journal of Theoretical Politics*, 4(3), 247–281.

McNicholas, C. and Poydock, M. (2019, November 14). How California's AB5 protects workers from misclassification. Economic Policy Institute. Accessed at www .epi.org/publication/how-californias-ab5-protects-workers-from-misclassification, November 18, 2021.

Medema, S. G. (2020). The Coase Theorem at sixty. *Journal of Economic Literature*, 58(4), 1045–1128.

Ménard, C. and Shirley, M. M. (Eds). (2005). *Handbook of new institutional economics.* New York: Springer.

Mollaneda, I. (2021). The aftermath of California's Proposition 22. *California Law Review Online.* Accessed at www.californialawreview.org/the-aftermath-of -californias-proposition-22, November 18, 2021.

Morris, M. (1992). Structure of entitlements. *Cornell Law Review*, 78, 822–873.

Nejaime, D. and Siegel, R. (2018). Religious exemptions and antidiscrimination law in Masterpiece Cakeshop. *Yale Law Journal*, 128, 201–225.

North, D. C. (1990). *Institutions, institutional change and economic performance.* Cambridge: Cambridge University Press.

North, D. C. (1991). Institutions. *Journal of Economic Perspectives*, 5(1), 97–112.

North, D. C. (1994). Economic performance through time. *American Economic Review*, 84(3), 359–368.

NRDC. (2021). Massachusetts Lobstermen's Association v. Raimondo. Accessed online at www.nrdc.org/court-battles/massachusetts-lobstermens-association-v -ross, November 18, 2021.

O'Connor v. *Uber Techs*, 82 F. Supp. 3d 1133 (Cal. 2015).

Ogaki, M. and Tanaka, S. C. (2017). Normative behavioral economics. In *Behavioral Economics* (pp. 185–207). Singapore: Springer.

Ostrom, V. (1976). John R. Commons's foundations for policy analysis. *Journal of Economic Issues*, 10(4), 839–857.

Ostrom, E. (1990). *Governing the commons: The evolution of institutions for collective action*. Cambridge: Cambridge University Press.

Ostrom, E. (2005). Doing institutional analysis digging deeper than markets and hierarchies. In C. Ménard and M. M. Shirley (Eds), *Handbook of new institutional economics*. Boston, MA: Springer.

Ostrom, E. (2008). Developing a method for analyzing institutional change. In S. S. Batie and N. Mercuro (Eds), *Alternative institutional structures: Evolution and impact* (pp. 48–76). New York: Routledge.

Ostrom, E. (2010). Beyond markets and states: Polycentric governance of complex economic systems. *American Economic Review*, 100(3), 641–672.

Oxford English Dictionary. (2020a). Definition of law. Accessed at https://www.lexico.com/en/definition/law, November 18, 2021.

Oxford English Dictionary. (2020b). Definition of rule. Accessed at https://www.lexico.com/en/definition/rule, November 18, 2021.

Pack, B. J. (2002). Regulatory takings: Correcting the Supreme Court's wrong turn in Tahoe Regional Planning Agency. *Brigham Young University Journal of Public Law*, 17, 391.

Peil, J. and van Staveren, I. (2009). *Handbook of economics and ethics*. Cheltenham, UK and Northampton, MA, USA: Edward Elgar Publishing.

Persky, J. (1993). Retrospectives: Consumer sovereignty. *Journal of Economic Perspectives*, 7(1), 183–191.

Pierson, P. (1997). Increasing returns, path dependence, and the study of politics. *Jean Monnet Chair Papers*. Robert Schuman Centre at the European University Institute.

Pierson, P. (2000). Increasing returns, path dependence, and the study of politics. *American Political Science Review*, 94(2), 251–267.

Potts, J. (2000). *The new evolutionary microeconomics: Complexity, competence and adaptive behaviour*. Cheltenham, UK and Northampton, MA, USA: Edward Elgar Publishing.

Proclamation No. 9496, 3 C.F.R. 262, 262 (2017). Accessed at www.govinfo.gov/content/pkg/DCPD-201600596/pdf/DCPD-201600596.pdf, November 18, 2021.

Reilly, A. (2019). Is the "mere equity" to rescind a legal power? Unpacking Hohfeld's concept of "volitional control." *Oxford Journal of Legal Studies*, 39(4), 779–807.

Roberts, R. (2012, May 21). Coase on externalities, the firm, and the state of economics. Audio podcast episode. *EconTalk*. Accessed at www.econtalk.org/coase-on-externalities-the-firm-and-the-state-of-economics, November 18, 2021.

Romo, V. (2019, May 15). Uber drivers are not employees, national relations board rules. Drivers saw it coming. *NPR*. Accessed at www.npr.org/2019/05/15/723768986/uber-drivers-are-not-employees-national-relations-board-rules-drivers-saw-it-com, November 18, 2021.

Rutherford, M. (1994). *Institutions in economics: The old and the new institutionalism, historical perspectives on modern economics*. Cambridge: Cambridge University Press.

Samuels, W. J. (1971). Interrelations between legal and economic processes. *Journal of Law and Economics*, 14(2), 435–450.

Samuels, W. J. (1972). In defense of a positive approach to government as an economic variable. *Journal of Law and Economics*, 15(2), 453–459.

Samuels, W. J. (2007). *The legal–economic nexus: Fundamental processes.* New York: Routledge.

Samuels, W. J. and Schmid, A. A. (2005). Costs and power. In N. Aslanbeigui and Y. B. Choi (Eds), *Borderlands of economics* (pp. 165–182). New York: Routledge.

Sant'Ambrogio, M. (2019). Private enforcement in administrative courts. *Vanderbilt Law Review*, 72(2), 425–500.

Schlag, P. (2015). How to do things with Hohfeld. *Law and Contemporary Problems*, 78, 185–234.

Schlager, E. and Ostrom, E. (1992). Property rights regimes and natural resources: A conceptual analysis. *Land Economics*, 68(3), 249–262.

Schmid, A. A. (1972). Analytical institutional economics: Challenging problems in the economics of resources for a new environment. *American Journal of Agricultural Economics*, 54(5), 893–901.

Schmid, A. A. (1987). *Property, power, and public choice: An inquiry into law and economics*, 2nd edition. New York: Praeger.

Schmid, A. A. (1999). Government, property, markets … in that order … not government versus markets. In N. Mercuro and W. Samuels (Eds), *The Fundamental Interrelationships between Government and Property* (pp. 233–237). Stamford, CT: JAI Press.

Schmid, A. A. (2004). *Conflict and cooperation: Institutional and behavioral economics.* Oxford: Blackwell Publishing.

Schmid, A. A. (2006). An institutional economics perspective on economic growth. Working paper, Michigan State University.

Schoenfeld, A. E., Walsh, J. F., Brown, R. J., Wolfson, P. R. and Gomez, E. F. (2017). Masterpiece Cakeshop, Ltd., et al., v. Colorado Civil Rights Commission, et al. Denver Metro Chamber of Commerce. Accessed at www.scotusblog.com/wp-content/uploads/2017/11/16-111_bsac_denvermetrochamberofcommerceetal.pdf, November 18, 2021.

Schweikhardt, D. (2016). *Institutional and behavioral economics course slides.* East Lansing, MI: Michigan State University.

Sen, A. (1987). *On ethics and economics.* Oxford: Basil Blackwell.

Sen, A. (1992). *Inequality re-examined.* New York: Russel Sage Foundation.

Sen, A. (1997). *On economic inequality.* Oxford: Oxford University Press.

Shah, P. A. and Cicconi, M. E. (2017). Amicus brief of chefs, bakers, and restaurateurs in Masterpiece Cakeshop v. Colorado Civil Rights Commission. *SCOTUSblog.* Accessed at www.scotusblog.com/wp-content/uploads/2017/11/16-111_bsac_chefs-bakers-and-restaurateurs.pdf, November 18, 2021.

Shapiro, I., Burrus, T. and Spiegelman, S. (2020). Cedar Point Nursery v. Hassid. CATO Institute. Accessed at www.cato.org/publications/legal-briefs/cedar-point-nursery-v-hassid-dec-2020, November 18, 2021.

Sichelman, T. M. (2018). Very tight "bundles of sticks": Hohfeld's complex jural relations. In S. Balganesh, T. Sichelman and H. Smith (Eds), *The legacy of Wesley Hohfeld: Edited major works, select personal papers, and original commentaries.* Cambridge: Cambridge University Press.

Simon, H. A. (1955). A behavioral model of rational choice. *Quarterly Journal of Economics*, 69(1), 99–118.

Thomas, R. H., Leong, D. K. and Hastert, K. (2020). Cedar Point Nursery v. Hassid. Southeastern Legal Foundation. Accessed at www.supremecourt.gov/DocketPDF/20/20-107/152014/20200902181625024_0000%20-%2020-107-Cedar-Point-v-Hassid-SLF-amicus-9-2-2020-final.pdf, November 18, 2021.

Uber BV v. *Aslam.* (2019). Court of Appeal, Civil Division, case A2/2017/3467. *Weekly Law Reports.* Accessed at www.iclr.co.uk/document/2017000496/casereport _65e21817-574d-4269-b2f8-c5a3d69df309/html, November 18, 2021.

Uber BV v. *Aslam.* (2021). United Kingdom Supreme Court. *Weekly Law Reports.* Accessed at www.bailii.org/uk/cases/UKSC/2021/5.html, November 18, 2021.

Urofsky, M. I. (2018, April 10). Lochner v. New York. *Encyclopedia Britannica.* Accessed at www.britannica.com/event/Lochner-v-New-York, November 18, 2021.

U.S. Department of Labor. (2021, July 1). Minimum wages for tipped workers. Accessed at www.dol.gov/agencies/whd/state/minimum-wage/tipped, November 18, 2021.

Vatn, A. (2018). Environmental governance – from public to private? *Ecological Economics*, 148, 170–177.

Verani, A. (2007). Community-based management of Atlantic cod by the Georges Bank hook sector: Is it a model fishery? *Tulane Environmental Law Journal*, 20(2), 359–379.

Voss, T. R. (2001). Institutions. In N. J. Smelser and P. B. Baltes (Eds), *International encyclopedia of the social and behavioral sciences* (Vol. 11, pp. 7561–7566). London: Elsevier.

Williams, S. J. (2003). Assets in accounting: Reality lost. *Accounting Historians Journal*, 30(2), 133–174.

Williamson, O. E. (1975). Markets and hierarchies: Analysis and antitrust implications: A study in the economics of internal organization. *University of Illinois at Urbana-Champaign's Academy for Entrepreneurial Leadership Historical Research Reference in Entrepreneurship.* https://ssrn.com/abstract=1496220

Wohlgemuth, C. and McDonald, D. C. (2020). Cedar Point Nursery v. Hassid. Mountain States Legal Foundation. Accessed at www.supremecourt.gov/DocketPDF/20/ 20-107/151904/20200902111448356_2020.09.02%20Cedar%20Point%20Cert. %20Pet.%20Amicus%20v.Final.pdf, November 18, 2021.

Yinger, J. (1998). Evidence on discrimination in consumer markets. *Journal of Economic Perspectives*, 12(2), 23–40.

Young, O. R., Webster, D. G., Cox, M. E., Raakjær, J., Blaxekjær, L. Ø., Einarsson, N. ... and Wilson, R. S. (2018). Moving beyond panaceas in fisheries governance. *Proceedings of the National Academy of Sciences*, 115(37), 9065–9073.

Zeigler, D. H. (1986). Rights require remedies: A new approach to the enforcement of rights in the federal courts. *Hastings Law Journal*, 38, 665–728.

Index